Know When to Hold, When to Fold . . . and Play Each Hand Like a Master

Zen and the Art of Poker will give you the edge as it improves your game and shows you how to:

Fit yourself into the flow of the game
Learn to use inaction as a weapon
Pick your times of confrontation
Master yourself, not the game
Take the long view
Play on instinct
Prepare for worst-case scenarios
Deal with losses, errors, and failure
Avoid self-defeating strategies
. . . and more

LARRY W. PHILLIPS is a journalist, writer, and longtime poker player. He has played poker most of his life and is equally comfortable competing with world-class or two-dollar players. He placed second in the 1997 Wisconsin State Poker Tournament.

zen
AND THE ART OF
POKER

Timeless Secrets to Transform Your Game

LARRY W. PHILLIPS

A PLUME BOOK

PLUME
Published by the Penguin Group
Penguin Putnam Inc., 375 Hudson Street, New York, New York 10014, U.S.A.
Penguin Books Ltd, 27 Wrights Lane, London W8 5TZ, England
Penguin Books Australia Ltd, Ringwood, Victoria, Australia
Penguin Books Canada Ltd, 10 Alcorn Avenue, Toronto, Ontario, Canada M4V 3B2
Penguin Books (N.Z.) Ltd, 182–190 Wairau Road, Auckland 10, New Zealand

Penguin Books Ltd, Registered Offices:
Harmondsworth, Middlesex, England

First published by Plume, a member of Penguin Putnam Inc.

First Printing, November, 1999

20 19 18 17 16 15 14 13 12

Copyright © Larry W. Phillips, 1999
All rights reserved

LIBRARY OF CONGRESS CATALOGING-IN-PUBLICATION DATA:

Phillips, Larry W.
    Zen and the art of poker / by Larry W. Phillips.
        p.   cm.
    ISBN 0-452-28126-1
    1. Poker—Psychological aspects.   2. Zen Buddhism.   I. Title.
    GV1255.P78   P55   1999
    795.41'2'01—dc21
                                        99-32700
                                        CIP

Printed in the United States of America
Set in Simoncini Garamond
Designed by Leonard Telesca

This book is dedicated
to Thomas and Patricia Sprain

Contents

IV. Warrior Zen

V. Emotions and Opponents

Appendix 1.

Appendix 2.

Sages follow the rules of heaven; the wise obey the laws of earth; the intelligent follow precedent. Harm comes to the arrogant; calamity visits the proud.

—Zhuge Liang

Who knows this morning what will happen tonight?

—Chinese proverb

zen
AND THE ART OF
POKER

Introduction

Be the ball.

—From the movie *Caddyshack*

The exotic mysteries of the East—of Zen Buddhism—coupled with the nuts-and-bolts psychology of cardroom poker? Images of Japanese gardens, wafting incense, and robed monks sitting in silence in . . . Las Vegas poker rooms? Enigmatic and elusive Zen wedded to tells, river cards, and rebuys? Is such a strange overlap of the two cultures possible? And if so, where—and at what points—do these two high arts intersect?

To the Western layperson, the most familiar example of Zen may come from the movies, or sports: the marathon runner who "runs within himself"; the golfer, bowler, or basketball player who is "in the zone," playing effortlessly, and so on. Such examples are, needless to say, superficial—hardly representative of Zen after a lifetime of training—but they do hint at a meaning.

A similar condition sometimes occurs in the game of poker. The great poker players, through a lifelong discipline at the game, eventually attain a kind of Zen state, one in which they are perfectly attuned to the rhythm of what is taking place in front of them.

Consider the following quote from poker writer Rex Jones:

All the great mystics of the world chose the middle path, the one between endless joy and endless suffering . . . The greatest mystic of them all, Gautama Buddha, knew that there were many methods of achieving enlightenment. Why not the game of poker? Poker has all the attributes of a great meditation technique. It's a mind game of the first order. It calls for a knowledge of math, psychology, strategy, tactics and self-discipline.

There is indeed an almost Zen-like state that takes place in poker, as the hours slip by and the game reaches a comfortable rhythm and the light changes in cardrooms and outside the windows of riverboats.

It is similar to the state of people who are in the thrall of some other activity—one that, for the moment, dominates them and justifies their existence. Such a hint of inner nirvana, at least for its devotees, could also be said to occur during poker.

On a practical level, as a tool, how effective is Zen? Is it a technique so powerful that it will guarantee to make you a winner? Will possession of the Zen state give you a vast secret superiority over other players? This approach looks at Zen the wrong way. Zen's influence is primarily on us. It can't influence outside events (except by example perhaps—calmness, patience, stillness, and so on, which others may see and adopt). It cannot *change* outside events. (It cannot change the cards.) We *will* still lose. However, it will give us mastery over ourselves—and in poker, this is crucial.

Certainly one of the most widespread failures in the realm of poker is emotional control. This is a failure so large that its impact rivals playing the wrong hands, not knowing the correct percentages, or raising and betting at the wrong times. Zen addresses this problem.

♥ ♣ ♦ ♠

Most poker players, by nature, would be unlikely to adopt Zen as a way of life, or as their primary philosophy. The notion of stillness, calmness, and patience, however, they *do* like—in a secondary way, as a tool—but not at the price of it being their primary lifestyle. Gamblers (and poker players), as a group, are generally celebrators, carousers, escapists, libertines, and libertarians; many of them operate with a half smile and a twinkle in their eye. The great majority love life too much to enter into any transaction in which denial, austerity, and self-effacement are major currency. (At the most advanced level, a certain monklike asceticism and dedication often do reign, however.)

Still, if there is some part of Zen that can help them, they are interested.

You may notice that some of the ideas in this book are similar to others. Their importance is great so they may be phrased in different ways and restated in slightly different forms and shadings. This, too, is Zen.

The points where Zen and poker touch or overlap (or even where Zen ideas begin to overlap with one another) are not always clear-cut. Like different sides or facets of a diamond, each idea represents a slight turn of the gem to the next facet, often bearing close relation to concepts that went before. There is, accordingly, some overlap and blurring that occurs, until the outlines of a larger picture emerges.

Any high-stakes poker game, especially among experienced players, is as much a ceremony as any Zen ritual. It is a carefully choreographed give-and-take of power, rhythm, parry, thrust, withdrawal, and retreat. Mastery and virtuosity appear. One of the central assumptions of Zen is that any activity can be raised to the level of perfection. Poker, as with other activities, fits this category. Let's begin.

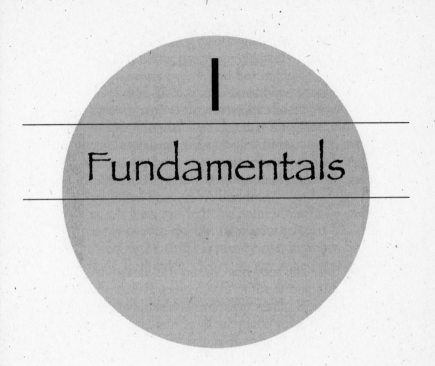

Fundamentals

1

What Is Zen?

Zen means awakening—awareness; to be awake in the present—in the moment. It comes from the Sanskrit word *dhyana* (pronounced *dee-yahna*), meaning "meditation." It is a tradition of Buddhism that originated in India, grew in China, and came to fulfillment in Japan—having been introduced into Japan by monks returning from China in the twelfth century.

Buddhism began 2,500 years ago with Gautauma, the Awakened One (Buddha) who, according to tradition, meditated under the bodhi tree at Gaya, in India, and achieved awakening. This awakening was of a simple nature—direct experience of reality, without thought or beliefs—and teachings based on this simplicity of viewpoint were passed down to a succession of disciples (called patriarchs) over the centuries. The twenty-eighth patriarch, Bodhidharma, carried the teachings to China.

We may have heard it said—perhaps jokingly—that someone is "at one with the universe." (Woody Allen once remarked that he was "at two with the universe.") The origin of this idea is that all things are connected. The only boundaries separating them are really in our own minds—the product of our beliefs and preconceived ideas. We look out at reality and endlessly label, categorize, and prejudge—

chopping it up into logical constructs, ideas, and formations, and it is because of this that the world appears to be separated and partitioned off. It is our loyalty to these beliefs that allows us to make fun of such a notion as being at one with the universe. But suppose for a moment that it was true? What if no partitions existed except the ones in our minds, the labels we have pinned on everything?

Rejecting such labels, Zen's belief is in an undivided wholeness of things and their constantly changing fluidity. It believes that seeking comfort in such labels is really a source of disaffection. It repudiates the endless grasping, straining, and striving that most of us do in the name of these labels and beliefs. To the outsider, such an approach may have the appearance of calmness, but it is really something deeper—what Zen calls *nongraspingness*, a belief in their non-necessity.

In Zen Buddhist tradition, many stories abound of youthful disciples applying to the master for entry into the monastery. In these parables, when the novice asks the master the secret of life, some mysterious, cryptic answer is always given—such as "the flower at midnight" or "three pounds of flax."

The purpose of such comments is to force the inquirer to concentrate, to really think about the answer, and finally to shock him into the recognition that it is thinking itself that is the problem: the answer lies beyond conventional thought. Buddhism's goal is to cut off the workings of the mind, to point out the flimsiness of these mental constructs we overlay onto all aspects of life. Seek reality directly is the suggestion, without words (*direct pointing*, Buddhism calls it).

As time goes on and we get older, we do get some inkling that the various labels we have put on the world are unhelpful, and they begin to fall away. With growing age and wisdom we let them go (in Western terms, we "mellow" as we grow older). Buddhism seeks to arrive at this realization sooner.

In light of this, the goal is not something that has to be sought; it is already within us. It is not something we look for or try to create, but a realization—of something already existing. The answer lies right around us, within reach.

Confucianism is a set of precepts, conventions, and rules for guidance in everyday life. It is focused on the *golden mean*. Zen has an aspect of this, too—a belief in the middle path, the ordinary way, neither being passive nor trying overly hard to dominate. It rejects these two extremes because it is in synch with, and moves *with* the world. It advocates a kind of harmony of balance.

This book is a collection of Zen quotes that apply to the game of poker, with comments in between. It had its genesis when I noticed how many Zen quotes seemed to apply to the game. Zen philosopher Alan Watts once wrote that he didn't think it was a good idea to import Zen to the West—the two societies and thought processes were too different—but that some ideas of Zen could certainly be used. That is my view with this book.

Does this book contain the wisdom of the East as applied to the game of poker? Yes. I really wanted to find something of value in the Zen doctrines for the poker player—not just a catchy title or a commercial hook for a book. I really wanted to conduct a search for substance, something usable that really did apply. This is the goal of the book.

My final destination (it turned out) was a single point that occurs, a psychological point of rhythm and instinct that is sometimes reached by the player—the "zone"—to try to get a fix on it and nail it down in words. As I discovered, however, it is elusive, and there are many roads that stream in from every direction that lead to this single point.

Lastly, I'd push for more interest in the process of the game than in the short-term goal of winning money in poker. The actual winning of money is not a tremendously difficult task, and can put some money in your pocket. But understanding the *process*, if done well, articulated well, can draw back the curtain on the whole affair.

The Differences Between Zen and Poker

There are some major differences between the Zen and poker lifestyles. It is probably unrealistic to think that poker players are ever going to adopt the Zen lifestyle in any fundamental way.

Here is a short list of Zen tenets that conflict with poker:

- Zen believes in banishing the ego. Poker players generally believe in the ego.
- Zen takes a dim view of verbalizing and explaining (Zen sees knowledge as something that is passed from "heart to heart"); Zen wants to stop the course of the mind—and empirical consciousness. Poker requires a certain amount of empirical reasoning.
- Zen believes in holy study, wisdom, and austere spiritual practices; it wants to drive out the impure heart. Many poker players have a pure heart. Others have an impure heart.
- Zen rejects the temptations of the senses and worldly pleasures—what Buddha called "the brigands of the five senses." Most poker players have partaken of, at one time or another, the brigands of the five senses.
- Zen embraces poverty. A belief in poverty is not the way for most successful poker players.
- Zen wants us to release self-will and desire. Most poker players are not very concerned with the dangers of self-will and desire.
- Zen tells us never to act selfishly and willfully. Poker players occasionally act selfishly and willfully.
- Zen believes that life is suffering. Poker players do not accept this—at least outwardly.
- Zen welcomes the void and believes in the "essence of fundamental emptiness." Poker players do not believe in the essence of fundamental emptiness.

Philosophically, the poker player and the Zen proponent are quite far apart—at least on the surface. My poker instruction took place mainly on the riverboats of the Mississippi. The masters I studied under there are closer to characters out of Mark Twain or Jack London than Gautauma Buddha, but each in his own fashion has arrived at his version of the "middle way." From the poker rooms of those riverboats the hills are visible on both sides of the Mississippi. Trains run alongside the river. On summer afternoons the sun gleams like diamonds on the river amid the buzz of speedboats and other activities. At night the moon shines on the water; at dawn the dark recedes and the sun comes up in the gradual grayness of half-light. In the distance the leaves change in autumn, and in winter the hills are in snow.

Inside the poker room, the dealer shuffles up, friends appear, players come and go, the game continues on endlessly. The individual player concentrates mightily, trying to discern the puzzle of the moment. The Buddhist might say the answer lies in the hills beyond.

2

Folding

You must learn to wait properly.
—Eugen Herrigel, *Zen in the Art of Archery*

This book is a calmative. Its theme is patience. But not patience of the usual kind—or even of the poker kind—but patience of the soul, and of the heart. While giving a respectful nod to the need for offensive play in the game of poker, this work's general thrust with regard to the game is quieter and more tempered, as befits Zen. This is not to say that it preaches passivity or that aggressive play is not required, only that, like Zen itself, a more balanced, detached approach is adopted. This viewpoint has deep roots in conventional poker wisdom as well (prudence, caution, tightness of play, among others)—roots which in turn have their source in a more mundane truth: In poker, you're going to be cold a lot more often that you're going to be hot.

Put another way, simply measured in quantity of hours, the times when your cards are running hot are going to be outnumbered by the times when they are running cold, average, and bad. And since this is the case, patience becomes a necessity—and a virtue.

How is patience translated into poker terms? For the most part, the answer can be summed up in a single word: *folding*. And this makes poker—at least a great deal of the time—a game of withdrawing, not the thrusting, attacking game that it may appear to the casual observer. Its long-term essence as an activity has certain parallels to a Zen state, therefore—a pulling back, a stillness, a non-activity. And while it is true that this pulling back always contains *within it* a nugget of aggression, an explosive core ever waiting to attack, a vast majority of the time it is of a more stationary nature. Until the player can make peace with this state emotionally, he cannot master poker.

One of the problems with the concept of folding, as an idea, is that the mind resists it, rebels against it—and this very fact makes it more difficult to grasp. If taken literally, it might lead to dialogue such as the following:

"Let's go over to the casino and fold hands for four or five hours."

"Let's drive over to the poker parlor and see how many hands we can stay out of."

"Let's go over to the riverboat and not play."

And so on. The Western mind, generally action-oriented, recoils at this sort of thinking; it has trouble grasping such an idea.

Indeed, it seems to go against the grain of logic. How can you win a game you drop out of? How can you win any competition you're not even in? After all, isn't being *in* the first step to winning? This is what the logical side of our brain tells us. Who ever saw a football team not take the field and win? Who ever saw a movie where the cowboy hero was playing in a poker game and was . . . folding? Folding? Of course not—he's in there *entering* pots, tossing in money, throwing his cards down, triumphing! He is certainly not withdrawing from the action.

This is why it is so hard to sell the concept (especially to new players) that over the long run the hands you fold make the hands you do play stand out more sharply and give them more power.

At any rate, the secret to poker—at least for the majority of players—could be summed up in three words: *fold . . . a lot.*

Most players, if they could keep these three words uppermost in mind (*and* act on them), would be light-years ahead of their usual game. This means playing only 15 to 20 percent of your hands (the *best* 15 to 20 percent) and throwing in the rest. A proper adoption of Zen principles—outlined later in this book—will help with this problem. And it is a serious problem. Known in card rooms as *playing too many hands*, it is the bane of poker players everywhere, even stretching to the upper levels of the top players. Why this would be such a difficult concept to master is a mystery, but its victims are legion, its effects epidemic. You will hear players say: "I know I should play fewer hands. *Mentally*, I know this. But I sit down at the table and something happens to me and pretty soon I'm right in there again, playing too many hands . . . I can't seem to stop myself . . . I keep doing it even though I know it's hurting my game."

One of the goals of this book is to introduce some helpful hints for this player.

POKER RULE #1: Learn to use inaction as a weapon.

As a weapon, in this war of poker, you have to teach yourself how to hit opponents over the head with your *inaction*. Inaction—folding—is one of the greatest, most powerful tools you possess.

In one sense, though, we're lucky. This great weapon of ours is something the other players *want* to see us do—withdraw—so it works out nicely. It is sort of an invisible way of winning. And make no mistake, this really *is* when you are winning.

This makes poker a difficult activity to dominate, however, because you do so by your ability to *back away* from the event. Very few events, games, or sports work this way, with the winner being the one who withdraws himself from competition at the proper moments.

You need to think of folding as a club you are using to pummel your opponents with. It is an odd club, admittedly, since it is one you *don't* use, but it is the club that will defeat them, over time.

To a large extent, the one who achieves greatness is the one who does *not* play—a Zen-like condition if there ever was one.

You must learn to allow patience and stillness to take over from anxiety and frantic activity . . . The good player is patient. He is observant, controlling his patience, and organizing his composure. When he sees an opportunity, he explodes.

> —Martial artist Jim Lau, quoted by Joe Hyams in *Zen in the Marital Arts*

POKER RULE #2: Don't get irritated or angered by long sessions of folding.

Come to the game expecting this. Accept it.

Rest assured that there will be an attempt (by the poker gods) to wear you down—to give you rag hands over and over, for extended periods of time. This *will* happen. And it will happen on numerous, and often successive, occasions. Know this ahead of time so you are mentally prepared for it when it happens.

POKER RULE #3: If you've been folding a lot, for a long time in the game, and you're starting to think that maybe it's time you got in and played a few hands again—that's not a good enough reason. Keep folding.

Just because you've been folding cards for a long time doesn't mean it's now time to start putting in money again on second-rate hands. Just because you've folded the last fifty hands doesn't mean you shouldn't fold the next fifty in a row if your cards aren't right.

Some players think there is some kind of invisible statute of limitations on folding. After two hours, you've paid your dues— you've proven that you're a disciplined player. So now you've earned the right to stay again, right . . . ? Nope. Keep folding.

There is interaction if there is a call for it, no interaction
if there is no call for it.
> —Zen master Yangshan

Develop a readiness to participate—that is, to explode into action—which is separate from the relaxed state you are in at the times in between.

When animals—and almost all normal people—face a
physical threat, their bodies go rigid. From a
physiological standpoint it's not efficient, but it's the
general rule. Polar bears are the exception. They can lie
in wait, perfectly relaxed, for two hours without once
releasing the heightened readiness of their muscles.
> —Peter Høeg, *Smilla's Sense of Snow*

POKER RULE #4: Don't feel like a martyr when folding.

Don't start feeling self-righteous about all this folding you're doing . . . as if now it owes you (because you've been so good, so disciplined, so patient . . .). This is a trap. Don't start to feel like a martyr from it. Such a feeling may seem innocent, but it is only one step away from playing again. As you keep folding, you must feel *neutral* about it.

Do you have the patience to wait
till your mud settles and the water is clear?
Can you remain unmoving
till the right action arises by itself?

—Lao-tzu

POKER RULE #5: Sometimes others get to play and you don't.

Sometimes in softball games, as a kid, they handed out the bats and balls and gloves and there wasn't enough to go around—so you had to *sit out*. You had to sit on the bench and watch.

The same thing happens in poker. Sometimes you don't get to participate.

You must get used to the idea that sometimes you will sit at the table for ten hours and nothing at all will happen. Others will have all the fun. There won't be enough bats and balls to go around. You will simply be riding the bench—watching.

But the most important thing is this: you must be comfortable with this—*welcome* it. Make peace with this idea. Cross your arms and sit back.

Always remember that the following scenario can take place:

All the good cards in the game can go to the player across the table from you for the first five hours. Then they can stop, just as suddenly as they started, and go to the player *next* to him for the next five hours—a scenario that leaves you completely out in the cold.

This is a plausible scenario. There is nothing far-fetched at all about it. The veteran poker player realizes when he sits down to play that there is a good chance that nothing at all will happen.

POKER RULE #6: To win at poker you must embrace the idea of breaking even.

No one sets out for a trip to the casino or the weekly poker game (or any form of gambling) with the idea of breaking even as a goal. Rather, we set out with high hopes, excitement, expectancy—the promise of big dreams. But then something odd happens when we get there—we break even. Our reaction is a feeling of annoyance, of letdown.

Breaking even happens. It is one of the possible outcomes. We must not see it as a nuisance or an unwelcome event. A distaste for breaking even can lead us into the valley of *pressing* and *overplaying* and other wrongful activity. Become comfortable with breaking even. Teach yourself how to sit quietly and patiently at the even mark.

You sit simply, as a warrior, and out of that, a sense of individual dignity arises.
—Chogyam Trungpa, *Shambhala: The Sacred Path of the Warrior*

POKER RULE #7: Regard patience as a central pillar of your game and strategy.

Think of patience as a primary part of your game. Don't assign it a secondary or lesser role. Elevate it on the list of what you consider important. Move it to a higher rung.

And don't be put off by it when it doesn't seem to be working. It's working . . . Beneath the surface, it's working.

Time opens every door to him who waits.
—Chinese proverb

POKER RULE #8: Keep plugging away. Expect nothing.

There will be times when you play tight, keep playing tight, and *keep on* playing tight, and it still does no good . . . the bad cards just keep coming. Remember: You don't get any award or gold star for this at the end of the night. You may have to just keep doing it until the end, with no reward at all.

This is a Zen state if ever there was one.

POKER RULE #9: Don't fall into the "Now Trap."

Newspaper headline:

MAN IS IMPATIENT! REFUSES TO WAIT!
MUST WIN NOW—NOT IN A HALF HOUR!
NOT INTERESTED IN WINNING A HALF HOUR FROM NOW!
MUST HAPPEN NOW! DOESN'T HAVE TIME TO WAIT!

This headline could apply to many of us in poker.

There is a great attraction in all aspects of the modern age to immediacy. It is very seductive in its lure.

Likewise, most of the trouble in poker occurs through this love affair with the "now"—with impatience, with trying to hurry up the game. Players want to win *now*, today. Results must happen now, in *this* hand, the one right in front of us.

We love the Now. We are devoted to it, infatuated with it, and give it much weight. (Note: This problem may be especially true if you have driven any distance to get to the cardroom or casino or have gone to a certain amount of trouble to get to the game. Then this slight pressure to play becomes almost palpable. You've driven all that way . . . you don't want to just sit there and fold cards, now that you're there. In fact, desperation of any kind can do this: joining a game that is about to break up . . . having only an hour to play . . . finding yourself down . . . or any combination of the above can tempt us into jettisoning our best game and jumping on the Now bandwagon once again.)

♥ ♣ ♦ ♠

There is a story about a group of Eskimos who are asked to draw a map of the area where they live. They draw a map of the outlying territory, and then they draw a large circle to represent the area where *they* live—a huge bulge in the center of the drawing that completely dominates the map.

We are all guilty of this. We assign a little more importance to where *we* are. We make it bigger, more important. Why? Because it is so much more significant than anywhere else. It has greater significance because *we* are there. But we do this *timewise,* too—we assign things more importance because they are happening in the present moment. Thus, if we were asked to draw a map of time, the *present* would have a similar bulge in the drawing—far out of proportion to its actual significance. Yet giving greater importance to the present in the game of poker allows us to imagine marginal hands into good hands and good hands into great hands.

POKER RULE #10: The long run is longer than you think.

Many poker players are smart enough to know that they will win over the long run by playing only the best hands, but they become impatient by the lack of anything happening. They forget that the long run can be *long.*

Playing only the best hands can be frustrating. They come along rarely, and even when they do there is no guarantee of winning with them. Long gaps occur in between. (We fold, the dealer shuffles for what seems like half an eternity, we get new cards, then have to fold again.) Anger and irritability can arise. The emotions can be severely tested. This is where Zen comes in.

Adopt the pace of nature;
her secret is patience.

—Ralph Waldo Emerson

POKER RULE #11: Don't defend patience too strongly.

One little-known error is that it is possible to defend patience too strongly. You can be too much in favor of it. The problem is that the concept itself is a soft concept. It is like the person who tries to force himself to go to sleep. You can't *make* yourself go to sleep through sheer strength of will. It is not about strength of commitment—it is more of a gentler thing—a *letting go*.

Being vehemently dedicated to patience is like being loudly committed to silence, or fiercely committed to gentleness.

Consider the following Zen quote on the best way to make yourself go to sleep:

All that is necessary is to lay down, not just the body, but one's heart and the whole of oneself.
  —Neville Shulman, *Zen in the Art of Climbing Mountains*

It is a letting go.
It is *not* a fierce commitment to letting go.
We must be able to back away from the game, but not by putting great commitment and the muscle of our emotions into doing so.

Some players unconsciously ratchet their emotions (read: *martyrdom*) up one more notch every hand they fold. So their emotions build, like steam pressure, to higher and higher levels. You can see the anger growing in them. They feel that by doing all this folding they are demonstrating superior poker ability—but they are not getting rewarded for it! When we inject emotion into folding it gradually builds up—like the steam in the steam engine. If we fold fifty hands in a row because we are getting bad cards, we should feel the same at the end of the fiftieth hand as we do after the first. We should feel neutral. In poker, patience means, not so much a strong commitment to patience, as an *indifference to the passage of time*. This indifference to *time* will in itself align you with a quiet and relaxed Zen-like state.

The finger pointing at the moon is not the moon.

—Zen saying

A ZEN RIDDLE: "The correct attitude . . ."

The correct attitude for the poker player is like a racehorse reined in. And by who? By himself.

But it is also the incorrect attitude.

(Calm and tranquility are better.)

POKER RULE #12: Don't be impatient about being patient.

We sometimes see a player who believes in patience, who has instructed his mind to play patiently, but not his emotions. His brain is telling him to play patiently while his emotions are saying, "What's taking so long?" These two must be in alignment.

A player should never come to the table with the idea of playing tight while also being impatient. These two are at cross-purposes. Such a player wants to play only the best hands, but he doesn't want to wait very long. He knows he must have patience, but he is very impatient about it.

POKER RULE #13: Occupy yourself while you're not playing.

You need to find other things to do while passing the time waiting for better cards. Try some of the following: help read the cards at the end of the hand; help split the pots; keep track of whose bet it is; watch how others play (and what cards they are turning over); look for "tells" (body language clues); start up a conversation with another player; listen to the jokes; go get the drinks and carry them to the table, and so on.

It is critical that you learn to enjoy yourself in the cardroom in ways other than in the game itself—by constantly staying, and playing. This is part of the Zen of withdrawing from the game that will help keep your game tight.

The fact is, if you are playing correctly, you are going to be doing a lot of folding. So you need to think of ways to fill this time. If you hate this period of time—when you're not playing, and some do— it will have the effect of throwing your game out of kilter.

POKER RULE #14: Learn to play against other patient players.

Sometimes a player who prides himself on his great patience has merely been playing in a game against less skilled players. He needs to ask himself how he would fare against a table of other patient players like himself. In this case, something quite unusual occurs. The game becomes a Gandhian contest of *non-action* with all the players trying to out "non-act" the others. In time, things grind to a halt. Nothing is happening at all. Players may be sitting around the table staring out the window, like non-acting Zen priests. There is no movement whatsoever. The waiting game has become so protracted, such a contest of Zen-like non-movement, that it seems like a waste of time.

This player discovers, to his surprise, that he only *thought* he was patient. Put in with this group he finds that there are other patient players like himself. He learns that there is a whole other level that exists. He learns that there is a patience so slow that it *is* almost Zen-like.

No thought, no action, no movement, total stillness.
                                                —Zen proverb

POKER RULE #15: Begin by playing tight, but don't forget to *stay* tight.

It is easy to *start out* playing tight, but then get caught up in the rhythm of the game—the table talk, the ebb and flow, the gossip, the laughter, the one-upmanship, the taunts, the chatter. And all of a sudden you notice that your chips are flowing into and out of the pot, all common sense has gone out the window, and you're in there with the best of them, flinging chips back and forth.

Some of this is occasionally necessary, in order to know how to operate within the flow of the game, but a lot of it is indulgent.

Catch yourself when you start doing this. Tell yourself to go back to more conservative play. The important thing is not who possesses the control and discipline at the *start* of the game, but who possesses it at the middle, the end, and all points throughout.

Wait for a good pitch to hit.

—Ted Williams

POKER RULE #16: Stick to the best starter cards.

One common method of playing tight is to play only good *starter cards.* (Starter cards are the player's first cards dealt to him in the game—the first three cards in Seven-Stud, the first four cards in Omaha, the first two in Hold'em, and so on. The list of these best starting hands is agreed upon by general consensus of pros and experts alike and is available in many poker books. An example of good starter cards in Seven-Card Stud might be a high pair in your first three cards—a pair of kings with a ten, say; or a medium pair with a high *kicker*—nines with an ace. In Hold'em, it might be a high pair or an ace-king suited.) Failing to play only good starter cards is like running a foot-race against the other players with a self-imposed handicap—like having a metal weight tied to your foot as the race begins. Play the best cards at the beginning of the hand, and the future will be a little less random, unpredictable, and murky.

One inch ahead is all darkness.

—Japanese proverb

POKER RULE #17: Learn to control chaos.

Chaos theory is the branch of physics that deals with situations that expand into disorder as they unfold. (This is a good description of poker—where things can get rapidly out of control.) One characteristic of such events is that they are sensitive to initial conditions. This means tiny differences or defects occurring at the beginning of the event become exaggerated as the event goes along. As the event unfolds it begins to branch out into greater unpredictability.

Only by avoiding the beginning of things can we escape their ending.

—Cyril Connolly, *The Unquiet Grave*

What this means for the poker player is that the best way to control chaos is at the beginning of the event. And the way to control it over a long-term period of time is to continuously repeat the beginning of the event in the same controlled way. Starting a poker hand with bad cards quickly branches out into unpredictability, and adverse effects begin. This is *not* readily apparent in actual play. It can be seen easily, however, in computer simulations of thousands of hands, where patterns quickly emerge. Playing a 7-10 in Hold'em, for example, might seem fairly harmless in the individual instance, but if you deal it out ten thousand times quickly on a computer you can easily see the disaster that unfolds.

There is nothing so subject to the inconstancy of fortune as war.

—Miguel de Cervantes

Wars, battles, and conflicts of all kinds (including poker) set in motion forces that quickly become unpredictable. Small defects or problems that are present at the beginning can quickly spiral out of control. And if small problems can do this, think what starting out with *large* problems means. Warlike conditions on any level unleash the chaos model. Wide fluctuations of fortune begin.

Accordingly, the rule is: Control things at the beginning. (This is what diplomats try to do.)

POKER RULE #18: Don't be drawn in by sudden frequent play on the part of another player.

If (contrary to the above) another player suddenly starts to play every hand, it's not because he wants to have more fun and wants to participate more, it's usually because he's getting better cards. Don't be drawn in by his seeming ambience and fun-loving spirit of jollity. Some players are very good at giving off this impression, a kind of nonchalance that seeks to leave the impression, "Heck, everyone else should be playing, too, just like I am"; or: "Hey, we're all just here to have a good time, so how come I'm the only one who gets to play every hand?" Implying that what they're doing is a typical stay rate and that all the other players are somehow playing too tight. (Another stratagem is continuous, forceful betting that makes it appear as if the player is trying to take charge of the game—muscle his way over the table—when in reality he is just getting good cards, that's the real reason for betting.)

As always, play *your* cards, ignore the actions of others.

Let others take their own way, and I take my own.
—Japanese proverb

POKER RULE #19: Discipline your game.

Discipline has some unfortunate connotations in the modern mind—it conjures up images of Marine drill instructors and strict regimens—but the word has a slightly different meaning in poker. It is more like patience—pacing yourself (especially emotionally) for the length of the game. It means detachment. Don't be drawn off your game. This is the Zen concept of retaining composure, being unaffected by outside forces.

It is different than mere patience, however. It comes from a larger and longer-term view of things—one that steps back and sees things as a whole.

One aspect of this patience is laying low during the cold spells, something that is crucial to conserving your chips during the bad times. It becomes easier to lay low when there is a lot of action taking place among the other players. (This lets you hide in the game and keep quietly folding without anyone noticing.)

Ideally, you want to be as invisible as possible when you are folding; slightly more well-known and memorable when you stay. Fold quietly and unobtrusively; be a little more talkative and animated when you stay. By this means you are playing tight while *appearing* to play a looser game.

3

Take the Long View

You must act as if the goal were infinitely far off.
—Eugen Herrigel, *Zen in the Art of Archery*

There is a saying in the poker world that "you play by the year, not by the day." This means taking the long view—judging results as they occur over the long run. Short-term upswings and downswings are disregarded, treated as unavoidable aberrations, and given little weight.

The average recreational gambler needs these short-term fluctuations. He enters a casino with a gleam in his eye, a hope, a dream, a lucky feeling, a rabbit's foot in his pocket. He needs the world of gambling to be a frenzied, chaotic world—one in which he jumps into the fray excitedly like a sailor on leave, then crawls back out later with a fistful of dollars.

This is the kind of world he wants it to be and needs it to be. But it is not. It is more like statistics and probability—the gradual emergence of correct play over the long run.

In a similar way, the real competition of poker takes place over the long term. Poker is basically a game of sitting and waiting for your theories on the game to be proven correct while waiting for your neighbor's theories to be proven wrong; this can take place only over time.

Many professional players have remarked upon this long-haul

aspect, calling it, as poker champion Bobby Baldwin once did, "one continuous game," which goes on forever and starts up again the next day.

Because of this, you don't defeat others in poker one-on-one, "heads-up" in a hand. (This is the way it may seem to a casual on-looker.) Rather, you defeat them on a hundred different occasions, each one matching up against the different moods and skills of the other, until the balance of one begins to slowly prevail over the other. It is your opponents' whole game matched against your whole game: from wide-awake, sharp, creative play to bad times and frustration to great spurts of good luck and folding for long stretches to drooping eyelids and exhaustion at six a.m. in the morning.

This domination by the better player of the lesser players is not a *dramatic* process, it is a gradual process.

Cream doesn't rise to the top,
it works its way up.
   —Harvey Mackay, from *Dig Your Well Before You're Thirsty*.

POKER RULE #20: "The true journey of mastery is in each moment."

Poker, much like Zen, must be applied to many situations over long periods until the whole framework of knowledge begins to fill in. It is a never-finished journey. New events, tribulations, and challenges arise. Just about the time we think we have the whole thing comfortably in hand, new obstacles come along to derail us.

The long journey (and learning) goes endlessly on.

Writer George Leonard, in his book *Mastery*, refers to this as the "goalless journey." In other words: there is no finish line; the journey itself is the destination.

A journey that has a specific goal or finish line has one benefit, of course: it makes that goal special once it is reached. The goalless journey, however, makes all the moments *along* the path special. According to Leonard, mastery lives within itself and the practice of itself—doing a thing for its own sake; not just reaching the goal, but each hour, each moment, every day is the goal.

POKER RULE #21: See poker as a continuum that goes on forever.

The game of poker should be seen as an endless plane upon which correct percentage play eventually prevails.

The idea is to avoid just throwing money around—to hold back until certain signals align themselves, until conditions are just right. *Then* jump in. Forget any desire or eagerness to participate in the action.

The winning gambler in any arena is the one who arrives with the idea of laying low, waits to get himself into good position, and then (and only then) makes his strike. He chooses his best spots, waits until the odds are most in his favor, then takes hit-and-run chunks of money, after which he takes disciplined steps to withdraw once again and avoid losing it all back. Players who operate like this are the ones who take home the money over the long term.

4

Practice, Practice, Practice

*The technically learnable part of it must be practiced
to the point of repletion.*
> —Eugen Herrigel, *Zen in the Art of Archery*

*Should you desire the great tranquility, prepare to
sweat white beads.*
> —Zen Master *Hakuin*

POKER RULE #22: You cannot apply the principles of Zen until you know the game perfectly—inside and out.

Having the proper attitude of Zen calm and confidence does
no good if you do not know the game. Zen will not make up for,
or offset, incorrect poker play. As a result, there is a certain
amount of ordinary, old-fashioned work involved in mastering the
game—a certain amount of sweating the white beads before the
days of tranquility come along.

The most important thing to know, above all things, is exactly
how to play the game. No outlook, attitude, or philosophy is as
important as this.*

Good poker is not a "mood," it is a series of individual deci-

---

*There may be *something* to be said about having a certain attitude: who hasn't seen a
complete novice sit down at the table with the attitude that "this game doesn't seem so
hard" and proceed to run over the game and pile up the chips? Well, this was an *attitude*
he sat down with, so maybe there is some kind of cosmic connection we don't understand.

sions. It does not occur by "Buddhistically" meditating ourselves into some dreamlike mental state, but rather by knowing the game well and being in synch with it—by inserting ourselves correctly into the flow of what is going on in front of us.

No Zen attitude will make up for this lack. You may be quite Zen-like and have all the attributes of Zen calm, but if you play incorrectly the result is that you will get destroyed. Practice, and long hours at the table, are indispensable.

Thousands of repetitions, and out of one's true self perfection emerges.
　　　　—Neville Shulman, *Zen in the Art of Climbing Mountains*

POKER RULE #23: Practice.

If you play tennis once a week against an opponent who plays tennis five times a week, who is likely to win? If you play chess or backgammon twice a year against someone who plays every day, who will mostly likely win? For some reason there are a lot of people who persist in thinking that poker is immune to this law. Keep in practice. It is a rhythm and a groove you get into, like anything else.

POKER RULE #24: Arrive with a system.

You need a system for poker play. The customary method of attaining this system is long hours of play, hard-earned personal experience, thinking about hands you've played and analyzing them, learning from your mistakes, a knowledge of probability, observing other players, discussing hands with other players, computer play, book learning, and any number of similar factors. Such a system will give you a correct mathematical and intuitive grasp of the game, and once in possession of this hard-won system, you should deviate from it only on rare occasions and for good reasons. (Such as, for instance, to randomize your play and throw your opponents off balance.)

Among other evils which being unarmed brings you, it causes you to be despised.

—Niccolò Machiavelli

Get the facts, or the facts will get you.

—Thomas Fuller

For the most part, there *is* a correct answer to almost every situation that occurs in poker (at least, mathematically speaking). You must find out from various sources (books and poker computer programs as well as the views of experts and fellow players) what these answers are and align your play with them as closely as possible.* This is important because these situations occur again and again. The more closely you align yourself with this statistically perfect game, the better you will do.

Once you attain this system it can operate almost by itself—the results will occur naturally. Once it is in place, you just do it, quite simply—almost neutrally—without thought of opponents or outcomes.

The spider dances her web without knowing that there are flies who will get caught in it.

—Eugen Herrigel, *Zen in the Art of Archery*

If your game is *not* complete, and has certain weaknesses, these weaknesses will eventually emerge.

You sometimes see this situation played out in cardrooms. You observe players who are making mistakes, playing the wrong

---

*Some of the finest work currently being done in this area is available in *Cardplayer* and *Poker Digest* magazines. The player is urged to subscribe. Also, Internet websites are available in which strategies are discussed and information is exchanged.

cards, and they are cheerfully winning, and then you see them on another occasion and they are cheerfully winning, and you see them on a third occasion and they are still winning, but then you see them on a fourth occasion and they are getting *destroyed*. Given enough time, the bad habits all come to the surface at once.

It is not enough to rely on luck or hope to carry us past the weak parts of our game. These parts must be attended to. The system must be whole and complete.

Zen itself functions out of wholeness. It does not turn a blind eye to uncomfortable parts. The weak parts must be corrected, or disaster will appear.

A small leak will sink a great ship.

—Anonymous

POKER RULE #25: Operate out of wholeness.

If you had to describe your toughest poker opponent, who would that person be? What qualities would he have? Take a moment and envision him. (This is important because this is the person *you* want to be, so you need to have an exact picture of him and what his qualities are.)

The answer is that he is someone whose game is *whole*—someone who seems to have a good hand every time he stays in the game; someone who plays aggressively and rarely loses; someone with a good-sized stack of chips and (apparently) unlimited money, who is unconcerned about calling a bet; someone who bluffs just frequently enough so others can never be quite sure of what he is doing; someone who knows all the exact values of the hands and can read his opponents well; someone who is unflappable and can't be rattled; someone who is calm, good natured, plays tight, plays equally well against few players or a full table, has almost no discernible body language, and plays with civility and courtesy.

Visualize this player. Then try to *be* this player. Work on making your game whole in this way, and as an opponent you will be difficult to lay a glove on.

———————————

Imagine a boxer coming into the ring, expecting to meet his opponent face to face. Instead, he finds himself in a ring filled only with fog. He swings wildly, but makes no contact with anything. His force is dissipating, and there is little he can do.

—Arthur Sokoloff, *Life Without Stress*

———————————

5

The Road to Eventual Mastery

POKER RULE #26: Learn from your mistakes.

If you make mistakes during the game, go back in your mind and see what you could have done better, or differently. There is usually something to learn from every game. For example, did you stay too long on one particular hand? Did you play too aggressively, or not aggressively enough? Should you have raised or re-raised in a particular situation, but didn't? Frequently this knowledge comes in the form of learning one more thing *not* to do.

Try to figure out what caused you to lose. Were you intimidated by somebody's aggressive betting? *Should* you have folded in the face of someone's aggressive betting, but didn't?

File away mistakes, mentally, and resolve not to repeat them. (One cautionary note: Don't use them to learn the wrong lesson, such as: "I'm a loser" or "I'm not very lucky." This is a common error. Some players use mistakes to *define* themselves, to beat themselves up. Instead, use them to move on *from*. Learn the correct lesson, then resolve not to repeat it.)

It is never too late to mend the pen after the sheep is lost.
—Chinese proverb

The truth is, mistakes don't matter much if you learn from them. Analyze mistakes, use them to adjust and move on to better play.

Large mistakes, horrendous mistakes, are usually self-correcting. Generally when we make one, we will not do it again. Mistakes always seem like failures at the time, of course (and always *feel* like failures), but they are really not—they are really a step forward.

There is always more learning to do in poker, no matter our level of play. The education is never complete. The journey goes on, with endless course corrections and continual adjustments.

The way goes onward and contains its own correction.
—Eugen Herrigel, *The Method of Zen*

Buddhism is not something one simply hears and grasps. It requires practice in which you rid the mind of impurities little by little.
—Suzuki Shosan, *Warrior of Zen*

The good player takes losses and errors as a constant lesson to readjust. The Zen Buddhist would say that when we factor past lessons in for future play, losses are *not* losses, but rather stepping-stones toward future correct play. Failure, by its nature, moves us in another direction, away from failure. We need to treat these lessons neutrally. Simply learn from them. Don't take them too much to heart or put too much emotion into them.

If defeat has more to teach us than victory, then perhaps a defeat is a victory unto itself?
—Miron Stabinsky, *Zen and the Art of Casino Gaming*

There are those who contemplate suicide in the bitterness of failure in life. But for a Buddhist this is pointless. When we fail, it is already progress to understand that we have failed. We train ourselves by making that failure a stepping-stone for a pace forward. The practice of Buddhism is to realize that the present success is the hundred failures of the past.

—Trevor Leggett, *A First Zen Reader*

II

Calmness and Rhythm

6

Calmness: Prepare for the Worst-Case Scenario

Forewarned is forearmed.

—Anonymous

Let's approach the idea of calmness from the other end of the spectrum first—impending disaster.

POKER RULE #27: Know all the ways you can lose big.

Heading off a bad night in poker is almost an art form. Knowing all the different ways you can lose is one way to guard against it (or at least to minimize it). Some of the ways you can lose include: a total drought of good cards all night long and being nickled-and-dimed and anted to death; second-best hands all night; second-best hands alternating with bad hands in between; hands that start out good but that don't "finish." And so on. Knowing these (and others) can give you some minor aid in heading off a disaster—at least you can begin to see its outlines ahead of time, before it appears in full force on the horizon. This is critical because how you deal with such occurrences can be the difference between having a bad night and having a full-scale, off-the-chart disaster.

POKER RULE #28: Know the range of what is likely to happen to you in a game.

In addition to knowing all the different ways you can lose, it is also helpful to know the general range of what you can expect to happen in a game—how cold things can get at their worst, how hot, and for how long.

For example, let's say the general monetary range of the game you play in is +$300 to –$300. These are the outside parameters of what you can expect to win or lose on any given night. If you know this going in, you won't be shocked and surprised by fluctuations that occur within that range. And this is important in keeping your mental equilibrium. It helps keep you in a state of Zen calm and composure. If you are familiar with these swings of fortune (–$300 to +$300), your behavior will be quite different from the player next to you who is down $200 and who is completely stunned, outraged, and indignant.

It's also important to know the *whole* range of poker outcomes—not just the maximum losing and winning amounts. There are many other intermediate outcomes. These might include:

- playing for six straight hours and being up $3;
- playing for ten straight hours against opponents who are not very good and being down $120;
- playing well and skillfully against a table of mediocre players and being down $300 after twelve hours;
- playing against very good players and being up $47;
- playing for two straight days and nights and being even;
- and so on.

There is an infinite number of outcomes that exist along the spectrum. Be comfortable with these intermediate outcomes, too. Do not be frustrated by them or think that they are somehow unacceptable. ("It's not possible I could be losing to this group of players"; or "It's not possible that I could be up only $5 after ten hours of play"; and so on.) You will note by observing the best players that they don't have a problem with any of these outcomes. They calmly accept them as they cash out and leave the table. Possessing such knowledge of the whole is a necessary part of the Zen attitude of composure.

POKER RULE #29: Expect the worst— why gamblers are pessimists.

By expecting the worst, you have already mentally dealt with it. You are ahead of it—steady, calm, cool, and collected for the next hand. The optimist in such situations fares poorly. Cheerfully expecting to win, he is stunned when it doesn't happen, and his agitation often carries over into future hands.

Thus, being a pessimist becomes a positive trait in poker. It allows you to forge ahead coolly. (And to *look* cool, too, which opponents often interpret as strength.) The ability to see the dark side—what can go drastically wrong—and to have this view of things always within easy reach become an advantage in poker.

POKER RULE #30: Don't expect a certain card to appear.

Bad players do this all the time—expect the best possible outcome to occur—and then are crushed when it doesn't. They are counting on a miracle card on the end to make their flush or straight or full house—their whole strategy depends on it—and when it doesn't happen, it's devastating. (A tip from more experienced players: Expect it *not* to come. You will probably be further ahead in the long run.)

POKER RULE #31: Don't get overconfident.

No matter how good we think we are or how many hands of poker we've played—whether one thousand or one hundred thousand—*don't* take that to the bank. Don't get overconfident, egotistical, arrogant. The reason: The Big Comeuppance can always be lurking around the next corner.

What is the Big Comeuppance?* It is similar to a lightning bolt that comes down out of the heavens. It wrecks your cards, hand after hand, hour after hour, even session after session. And it can start at any time. Egotism or arrogance have no place in any process where this can occur. *Humble* is the watchword here.

Don't begin to walk too tall when things are going well. Humility is a central aspect of Zen.

Pride means the end of wisdom.

—Japanese proverb

Pride goeth before destruction, and an haughty spirit before a fall.

—Proverbs 16.18

Let's repeat it, because it is so important: the Big Comeuppance can start at any time. It can begin on the very next hand. What is it like? It is like one of those days when you go to use a stapler and it is out of staples; and then you go to use a tape dispenser and it is out of tape. And then you pick up a flashlight and the batteries are dead. Then you use an elevator to reach the twentieth floor of a building and some kid has punched every button so the elevator has to stop at every floor. Then you dismiss all of the

------

*This label and others like it—the Big Meltdown, the Sky Falling In, Your Worst Nightmare—may seem overly dramatic, even melodramatic, until you are going through it, that is. When you are in the midst of it, the concept has a very accurate ring to it indeed, and the name will seem quite apt and fitting.

above from your mind and sit down calmly to tie your shoelace and it breaks off in your hand. The rest of the day proceeds in a similar fashion. There are days in poker that closely match this scenario. (And they can be the start of weeks or even months.) They can begin without warning and can go on indefinitely.

Be on your guard. Be vigilant. Arrogance has no place in any situation where this can occur.

———————

Boast not thyself of tomorrow; for though knowest not what a day may bring forth.

—Proverbs 27:1

There is an uphill road and there is a downhill road.

—Japanese proverb

———————

POKER RULE #32: Learn how to avoid a losing streak.

Is there anything you can do to avoid a losing streak? There are a few things.

First, watch for *any* clues that you might be getting cold. And by this I mean *early* clues. (Your starting cards are consistently terrible, or you have good hands that keep coming in second, or you seem to "hit a wall" every time you make any kind of move in the game, or whenever you do get good hands they only win a quarter of the pot, and so on.) Don't let losing over and over at the end of the hand be your *first* clue that you're cold.

One of the difficulties with a losing streak is that it is not a losing streak until it happens. That is, you're not really down until you're down—and then it's too late. Its very essence is a combination of events that takes you suddenly beyond the shore and drops you there before you can prepare for it.

Here is an example: You're down $170 after a series of unfortunate hands, but now you're in a big pot with a very good hand, so if you win you'll be approximately even. But a miracle card comes on the end for your opponent and you lose again and now you're down $290. Sitting there a moment later, you wonder to yourself: How did it happen? How did I get so far down and not see it coming?

One answer is: You weren't there until you were there. And then it was too late.

But there is a second problem here as well: you can't structure your game around this sort of thing happening. To design your game too much for this would be poor play and would stunt your game. So, in a sense, you *have* to be unprepared for it.

Look for early clues; they are sometimes the harbingers of worse things to come.

The fall of one leaf heralds the coming of autumn.

—Chinese proverb

POKER RULE #33: When things start going right for other players and wrong for you, back off.

This would seem to be so obvious and self-evident that you'd think every player would do it instinctively, without even thinking about it.

But do they? Do they back off? It's astonishing how many players step *up* their involvement at this point.

Ego usually plays a part in this.

In fact, the easiest thing in the world is to reach for your ego at this point. To bet right into the situation. Go up against it, challenge it. After all, things were going so well for you just a little while ago.

The probable explanation for this is that we are endlessly optimistic. Few players are convinced after three or four second-place finishes in a row. It can't happen again. It simply can't. Things are bound to turn around. Looking back at the end of the night, however, at how a losing streak was put together, certain things stand out, and this is one of them: we should have caught on a little sooner. It is important that we notice these situations earlier and react accordingly.

Bad Luck—When the Cards Are Not Running Well

It has been observed that players actually play worse when their cards (and luck) are running badly. (This also inspires opponents to play better, seeing us struggling.) For this reason, losses hurt *doubly* when they occur. Oppositely, most people begin to play better when things are running well, so they enjoy a double benefit: good luck *and* good play. It is for this reason that there seems to be an almost exponential difference between the two states—one that goes beyond merely the difference between winning and losing—and why they sometimes seem like they are worlds apart, almost like two different games.

7

Calmness:
The Ordinary Way

POKER RULE #34: Detach yourself emotionally from the game.

The game of poker is nothing more than a long, random, neutral statistical run, one that is predictable for the most part, with occasional aberrations in between.

Every experienced player knows the following truth: the four jacks he loses to heartbreakingly one week are quite likely to reappear in his own hand two or three weeks later for a win. Everything evens out. This is why getting angry, pounding the table, throwing the cards, and so on is pointless. In fact, it is worse than pointless, because still-heated emotions often lead to bad decisions on subsequent hands (attempts to "catch up" quickly or "get even" with somebody, or to "win it all back quickly" or "push a mediocre hand through" out of sheer stubbornness—or any variation of the above). In such a situation, a cloud of emotions takes possession of the player, commandeers his brain, and disrupts his play.

The action and repose of those who have mastered Zen are like flowing clouds . . . People who have mastered Zen are not stopped by anything: though clearly in the midst of all things, still they are highly aloof.

—Zen master Hongzhi

As regards the quietude of the sage, he is not quiet because quietness is said to be good. He is quiet because the multitude of things cannot disturb his quietude.

—Chuang-tzu

Remain dispassionate. Make it your goal to achieve a cool and calm demeanor. This is necessary in order to "keep the airwaves clear" in order to read incoming signals correctly.

You must function independently of what occurs on the table in front of you. Don't let your poker play be determined by passing moods.

When the pools of perception are cleansed, everything appears as it is.

—Zen proverb

Everything is based on mind, is led by mind, is fashioned by mind. If you speak and act with a polluted mind, suffering will follow.

—Buddha

Many aspects of poker are quite subtle and complex—more so than they may appear. Many gray areas exist, many borderline decisions. Superheated emotions can tip all these borderline decisions the wrong way, like dominoes, until they add up to disaster. Skill at detachment (and rebounding from losses) is important; the ability to dismiss the previous hand from mind is crucial. If this is not done the mind has as its principle *focus* this angry red cloud of emotion. It will see in its anger only this red cloud. How can the mind make accurate playing decisions when it is staring through a red cloud?

Also (as if this isn't bad enough), emotions in poker become connected to the cards and opponents can begin to read you. (Studies by psychologist Paul Ekman have shown that the stronger the emotion, the harder it is to conceal.) Opponents easily start to make a connection between your cards and your expressions.

Please don't think . . . that I am showing off when I say that I know the secret of how not to lose but win. I really do know the secret; it is terribly silly and simple and consists of keeping one's head the whole time, whatever the state of the game, and not getting excited. That is all, and it makes losing simply impossible . . . But that is not the point: the point is whether, having grasped the secret, a man knows how to make use of it and is fit to do so. A man can be as wise as Solomon and have an iron character and still be carried away.

—Fyodor Dostoyevsky

One method of remaining calm is by detaching yourself emotionally. Be as indifferent as possible to the outcome of the hand, knowing in advance that aberrations (in the statistical long run) are going to occur. Put your focus on playing your cards correctly, not on the emotional fluctuations of your fortunes. (The question arises: Do good poker players ever get angry? Yes, they do: when these aberrations occur eight or nine times in a row; when loss follows loss, hour upon hour—even day after day—things can get extremely irritating, Zen or no Zen; when hands that could go either way keep falling the other way, toward the other players; when this is coupled with long dry spells in between; and—let's take it one step further—if the whole thing is topped off by happening numerous *sessions* in a row. Such a scenario can be downright debilitating, and it becomes difficult to remain neutral and detached. A feeling of indignation arises—a smoldering feeling in the pit of the stomach. It is hard for Zen or anything else to cope with this.)

Yet, detachment must be retained. It must always be a high priority. It is easy, of course, to be in a Zen state of ease and relaxation when you are winning (in fact, this *is* the Zen state—when things are going well). The trick is to be in it when you are struggling.

Take a step back from the game. Try to see both good times and bad with a detached, neutral eye.

While the bad times can be frustrating (and sometimes even devastating), you must realize that getting yourself beyond this, emotionally, is the edge you have over other players (who will self-destruct when their turn at this happens).

You should let go and make yourself empty and quiet, clear and calm.

—Zen master Ying-An

Profoundly stable and calm, like a gigantic mountain, you cannot be disturbed by cravings or external conditions.

—Zen master Ying-An

POKER RULE #35: Develop a true indifference to the game.

George Leonard writes in *Mastery* that mastery's true face is often "relaxed and serene, sometimes faintly smiling." You sometimes see this with good poker players—a kind of smiling, ironic indifference to the vicissitudes of fate and the outcome of hands. Importantly, however, this is a true indifference. They are not pretending; it is not some kind of "act." Such a player watches the event almost as he would a contest in which he has no vested interest.

This kind of indifference is very valuable in poker. It helps keep resetting us back to our best game, no matter how horrendous the outcome of the previous hand. It is also valuable for another reason: it doesn't register on the face or body language, for the player always tends to look composed and unconcerned. (A note regarding this indifference: You obviously have to care enough to be focused on your play during the game. This isn't the kind of indifference where you aren't paying attention to what you're doing. That sort of indifference *will* result in money losses. Indifference to the *outcome* of hands must be kept distinct from indifference during actual play.)

Everything that happens, and above all what happens to me, should be observed impartially, as though on the deepest level it did not concern me.

—Eugen Herrigel, *The Method of Zen*

This is the point you want to get to: a detachment so complete that it almost borders on disinterest. (Cautionary note: It is important to have a large enough bankroll to allow you to play like this.*)

Over the long run, let's say, you know that a certain bet will work out in a certain card game situation—that it will show a profit. That is all you are interested in. So, in a sense, you really *don't* care what happens. You bet away—almost mechanically—as if the cards themselves are betting and you are not involved. This is the kind of approach that operates out of a base of Zen calm.

Employing this method allows us to respond to calamities in the game neutrally, to not dwell on them or exaggerate them unduly. This detached viewpoint works in our favor over the long run.

It is a matter of . . . living in the midst of passions yet being detached from passions.

—Zen essence

---

*Clearly, the reason for much of the stress and anxiety occurring in poker is a short bankroll. This stems from a kind of paradox: In order for a win to have meaning, we over-play our bankroll. But this in turn brings the annoyance/anger factor into play and takes us off our dispassionate, detached view.

Enter the game neutrally and exit it neutrally at whatever point you are ahead or behind.

(You won't really do this—in actual practice—but this hints at the demeanor you need to have, the state of mind that is called for: a neutrality almost bordering on arbitrariness.)

POKER RULE #36: Don't take the game personally.

The poker gods are not out to destroy you personally (although it may sometimes seem that way). The game itself is as neutral and mechanical as a roulette wheel, a church raffle, or a lottery ball drawing. A poker deck does not have any personal feelings one way or the other toward you or anyone else. At various times, we may rest assured, everyone "gets his," while at other times we are dealt miracle cards that pull out a miraculous victory at the last moment. Realize ahead of time that both outcomes are going to occur.

Everything is true just as it is: Why dislike it? Why hate it?

—Zen proverb

A return to Zen is a return to calmness. We must always remember that all that is necessary is to just sit there. This *is* all that is necessary. Nothing else is required. Remember that poker is a pastime—in the literal (as well as the Zen) sense—and must be seen as such. Stop straining in a hundred different directions. Stop looking endlessly for other and better situations. No other thing is needed.

Sitting quiet, doing nothing, spring comes, and grass grows by itself.

—Zen proverb

Players sometimes think that great things are called for—sophisticated plays, plays that go beyond the ordinary, into the extraordinary, where some other realm of effort is required. In fact, once skill is achieved, ordinary levels of calm are sufficient.

In Zen we are always told . . . to leave the danger of the high places and go on the path of safety. That path means just ordinariness . . . To be able to return and settle *in normality is the final stage of Zen.*

—Trevor Leggett, *A First Zen Reader*

The ordinary way is the way.

—Zen proverb

To repeat: players often think that elaborate steps are needed—great straining, striving steps, complex steps. The ordinary way of Zen dispels this. In modern life, as in poker, we often find ourselves tangled in frantic activity, trying to force events to our will, to *make* them happen. The actual answer is much simpler and involves a more natural approach. This sort of simplicity has been described in Zen literature in the following way: "When hungry, eat, when tired, sleep."

In Buddhism there is no place to apply effort. Everything in it is normal—you put on clothes to keep warm and eat food to stop hunger—that's all.

—Zen master Yuansou

The same may be said of poker.

In walking, just walk.
In sitting, just sit.

—Zen master Yun-Men

The ordinary way is the way.

8

Detachment: The Ego-less State

Attachment is the great fabricator of illusions; reality can be attained only by someone who is detached.
—Simone Weil

Nonattachment is the outstanding quality to be sought in applying Buddhism to our modern daily lives.
—Arthur Sokoloff

POKER RULE #37: Nonattachment.

The idea of attachment, in Buddhistic terms, means the linking of our emotions with something that we want—some desired object or outcome. The stronger this connection, the more discontent when we fail to achieve our ends (as well as desperate steps taken trying *to* achieve them). In the doctrines of Buddhism, this is one of the great sources of dissatisfaction in life—the beginning of disappointment, desire, envy, expectations, frustration, and so on. Dissolve this connection (the theory goes) and a more serene person results.

This Zen concept of nonattachment is at odds with Western notions. For instance, the Western idea of fun and excitement: if something is stimulating or fun or exciting (whether a golf match, auto race, or poker tournament), and we find ourselves getting emotionally drawn into it, then by definition *caring* starts to come into play. At this point, our detachment begins to fade. Also, any time we spend a lot of time doing any activity, we naturally begin to care about it, which makes detachment harder to achieve. (Ironically, detachment in poker becomes somewhat easier if we get away from the game for a while, but then our skills deteriorate slightly.)

This is also one of the areas of common ground that exists between Zen and poker. How much should we attach ourselves to our goals and objectives in poker?

Poker expertise (at least emotionally) could be said to exist at the point where caring and not caring intersect.

The Way is not difficult; only there must be no wanting or not wanting.

—Chao-Chou

Teach us to care and not to care
Teach us to sit still.

—T. S. Eliot

It is your personal system (developed over long hours of poker play, and experience) that is really what is sending chips into the pot. It does so coldly and mechanically, in response to various game situations. Your cards are playing the hand. But there is a hitch. Your *emotions also* have a free hand to do this, to send chips into the pot. This interloper, this troublesome meddler, is given free rein to do the same thing, and can therefore throw a wrench into your hard-earned system. Thus it is necessary to keep a watchful eye on this latter element.

While it is true that our emotions are also free to send chips into the pot, always remember the following:

Emotions have no place in poker.

You want to see some emotion on your wrestling team; you want to see it on the gridiron with your football team or on the ice rink with your hockey team, and in many other sports and activities. Wanting to win more than the opponent is important in these activities. But it serves little purpose in poker. Some of the worst players you will encounter while playing poker will be of the emotional variety. (Some of these people may be confusing the activities above with poker—attempting to carry over the attitudes they learned in sports. It is how they were trained to compete. But it doesn't work here.)

With the exception of such secondary emotions as confidence in your game, respect and enjoyment of fellow players, satisfaction at having played well, later (or conversely, disappointment), caring enough to focus and play well, and the fun or social aspects of it, emotions have no place in the actual playing of the game itself. They are simply a detriment and cause distortions.

One thing that makes this difficult, of course, is that emotions were how we got hooked on the game in the first place—the surge of winning, the thrill of the game, the feeling of victory, and so on. Because of this, emotions are intimately *bound up* in our mind with the game in its original form, as we first knew it, and our enjoyment of it. And this makes it difficult to extricate oneself from it later.

(As for the will to win, which some would say is a necessary emotion—and is certainly present in all the great players—it may be said that while this is an advisable emotion to possess, it ought not to be relied upon too heavily.)

You must not be astonished at anything that comes up . . . Accept it all calmly, as if you were a mere spectator, uninterested, and were observing a process for which you need not feel responsible . . . The result, in the end, is perfect stillness.
                                    —Eugen Herrigel, *The Method of Zen*

Ego-less Aggression

The majority of poker players, if asked, might think it would be impossible to play in what Zen calls "an ego-less state," but this is not the case. To play in an ego-less state means simply to not let the ego and emotions get involved. This type of detachment makes someone else's victory over you slightly unsatisfying—almost a neutral event.

Indeed, it is hard to get the upper hand on someone in a poker game who seems not to care—or appears to be indifferent to the outcome. Likewise, your victories, too, are hard to envy or resent because you play quite neutrally, never complaining when you lose.

This is the soul of ego-less aggression. To be aggressive without doing so in an ego way requires a mechanical, almost robotic response to situations.

Get no joy, except a superficial joy, out of winning. Get no sadness, except a superficial sadness, out of losing. Get to the point where it must almost be an act on your part to be joyful or to be sad—and not the opposite, as it is with most people.

You should not grieve over bad shots; learn now not to rejoice over the good ones. You must free yourself from the buffetings of pleasure and pain, and learn to rise above them in easy equanimity . . . This too, you must practice unceasingly—you cannot conceive how important it is.

—Eugen Herrigel, *Zen in the Art of Archery*

POKER RULE #38: Don't accept your opponents' idea of nervousness.

Sometimes you are in possession of calm and composure but your opponents unwittingly suggest—or project—a kind of nervousness upon you. This odd condition, which might be called "sympathetic nervousness," falls under the peculiar category of getting nervous because your opponents think you ought to be. (A $10–$20 player is suddenly thrust into an exceedingly "tense" moment, say, in a much smaller $1–$4 game.) All the other players are on the edge of their seats, staring at you, waiting for you to make your play. You're *supposed* to be nervous at this moment. This nervousness is supposed to be contagious, somehow.

You may get to a point (because of this) where it is not your emotions anymore that are the problem—it is your opponents'. Theirs resurrecting yours—or trying to—ghosts of former emotions you no longer have. A kind of willed tension around the table is focused on you, as if signaling to you that yes, *now* is the time for you to be anxious and uptight, almost demanding that you become as tense as they are. (Some players may even *want* you to fall for this gambit, for their own reasons.) In the calm you possess, however, you must break this spell, too.

Solution: Realize the detachment of your inner calm. Maintain your true indifference.

POKER RULE #39: When you take your emotions out of the game, other players' emotions become visible.

When we are focused exclusively on our own emotions (as we often are), the emotions of others tend to be obscured. When we make ourselves neutral, however, we find that the canvas suddenly becomes blank and the emotions of others begin to appear.

When the "I" is eradicated, that is the true Dharma.
                                    —Arthur Braverman, *Warrior of Zen*

9

Naturalness: The End of Self-Frustrating Effort

You are luckily all right by yourself, yet you struggle artificially.

—Zen master Dazhu

Steve Hagen, in his excellent book *Buddhism Plain and Simple*, gives us the example of a maple leaf falling on the ground under a maple tree and joining the natural pattern of other leaves that have fallen there. He asks us to imagine how difficult it would be for willful action on the part of humans to create such a pattern—requiring struggling, planning, effort, and toil—a pattern that is quite naturally and effortlessly created by nature.

Saul Bellow was getting at much the same thing when he wrote that "when the striving ceases, there is life waiting as a gift." In Buddhistic terms, when the struggling ends, things often reach a more effortless state.

The same thing occurs in poker. When you finally become a good poker player and look back at your early days, you will see that often you were pressing. You were like a person trying to force the maple leaves into a pattern, when it was naturalism that was required all along. You were probably overplaying; there was no harmony to your actions. You were not attuned to the rhythm of what was going on, the game in front of you, or yourself within the game. Your emotions were probably under dubious control, you weren't reading the other players very well (and they were probably reading *you* very well), and you were likely playing the wrong cards. Even though in a technical sense you may have been playing correctly at times, there was no real *soul* to your game—you were missing opportunities that were occurring within "the flow."

The beginning player who is currently in this situation may sometimes speculate what he will be like someday as a good player. How will he think then? How will he play? He tries to project himself ahead to those far-off days. It is not likely he will stumble upon the answer by accident, however, for it only arrives after long experience. You find that once you learn the game well, and stop pressing, stop trying to bull your way through, and get into the rhythm and flow of it, it arrives magically, as if by itself. A Zen-type rhythm has been reached.

Samsara is the circle of self-frustrating effort . . . it is essential to break out of this circle in order to obtain achievement.
—Neville Shulman, *Zen in the Art of Climbing Mountains*

Another way of putting it is: You will hit, simply by accident, after ten thousand tries at something, a rhythm that you could never have hit on purpose after only a few tries.

Long-time experience is the best teacher.

From the moment we cease trying to swim upstream and begin to flow with the current, something changes within us.
—Arthur Sokoloff, *Life Without Stress*

When the way comes to an end, then change. Having changed, you pass through.

—I Ching

You may sometime stand in the distance in a cardroom and watch pro players at a poker table and wonder what they are thinking, what is going on in their heads. But then a day will come when you will be playing and you will notice someone else looking at you in the same way and you will realize that now you've switched roles. You have passed through to the other side.

The more advanced level of poker is hard to describe. Even world-class players have difficulty putting it into words. By the time you attain a high level of technique you probably won't be able to explain what it is, either. (You won't be able to explain it back to your earlier self.) It is more of a feeling, a sixth sense; mainly of everyone moving one way so you move the other; an instinctive grasp of the drift and movement of game situations—when to back off and when to push forward.

It's just like learning archery; eventually you reach a point where ideas are ended and feelings forgotten, and then you suddenly hit the target.

—Zen master Ying-An

POKER RULE #40: Play "within yourself."

Like an Olympic runner who learns to run "within himself," you will eventually become comfortable inside your knowledge of the game. You will cease striving; the clouds will disperse, the sun comes out.

Even if our efforts of attention seem for years to be producing no result, one day a light that is in exact proportion to them will flood the room.

—Simone Weil

Where You Want to Get to As a Player

You will always still lose in poker, no matter how good you are at the game.

But your goal as a player is to reach the point where a great many things will have to go wrong for you to lose badly. They will have to go wrong in bunches, repeatedly, for an extended period of time. Once you have reached this point, you won't give it as much weight because you know that such occurrences are relatively (and thankfully) rare.

POKER RULE #41: Master yourself, not the game.

It is also important to come to the table with the goal of mastering yourself, not just the game. In many ways, this is more important than mastering the game. The reason is simple: For the most part, you already know the game. This mastering of yourself, however, is the work of a lifetime.

In many poker games you will play in, the skill level of all the players will be approximately equal. No one at the table will have a great advantage over anyone else. Therefore, the main edge that you have will be the mastery of yourself.

Self-control is part of Zen.

Morihei Ueshiba, the founder of Aikido . . . realized that the truly critical struggle in man was not physical combat, but rather the internal confrontation with the forces that lead him out of harmony with the spirit of the universe.

— Chuck Norris, *The Secret Power Within*

Falling Off the Zen

Occasionally players who play well and who are generally in harmony with what is going on (and who, we might add, know better), fall *off* the Zen, and when they do, they sometimes fall hard. Their natural self-control and composure gets, for one brief moment, suddenly and annoyingly old (similar to the person who has been on a diet for a long time and suddenly loses it and embarks on a desperate eating binge). The harmonious Zen individual is no more. The formerly mellow individual is a memory. A type of anger not unlike childishness gains the upper hand.

The former Zen player is now a fuming player. He may deliberately go down the list and do exactly the opposite of everything he knows he should be doing—willfully, almost spitefully.

This is what is known in the poker world as *tilt.*

Tilt can be the result of bad luck, bad *beats* (tough losses on very good hands), lack of emotional control, playing too often, or any number of other factors. It's hard even for a veteran player to be at the top of his form in every game, all of the time.

There is also a danger if you have been relatively hot for a while. You become too accustomed to things working. And then suddenly they don't. Annoyance sets in—and irritability. You're playing just as you were before, only now you're losing. The game itself begins to seem like a waste of time.

What is needed is a return to Zen. All methods of forcing, striving, and straining must be rejected—naturalness embraced. We must step back, see the big picture, and try to get ourselves composed again.

Zen always reminds us of the need for patience, not forcing things. While it cannot control outside events, it can lead to mastery of yourself, which in turn will begin to control your game—and indirectly, their game.

POKER RULE #42: Your biggest opponent, and worst enemy, is always yourself.

Years of experience eventually teach you that your main battle, always, is with yourself—your propensity for errors, for rationalizing marginal hands into good hands, lack of concentration, misreading other players, emotional eruptions, impatience, and so on. Your opponents are merely dim outlines that come and go. Few of them ever reach the exalted heights of damage that you can inflict on yourself.

10

Rhythm: The Back-and-Forth Flow

An ancient said: "The mind turns in accord with all situations; this turning is truly mysterious." The Master said: "Recognizing your nature in accord with the flow" means that if you want, you take; and if you are slapped, just be slapped. If you follow the flow in this manner, [the mind] will turn in accord with all situations."

—Suzuki Shosan, *Warrior of Zen*

POKER RULE #43: Be wary of pushing forward aggressively when encountering resistance.

There is a well-known rule of warfare: "Advance with bayonet; if you encounter mush, proceed; if you encounter steel, fall back." Contrary to this maxim, many poker players push forward and, encountering steel, what do they do? They *keep* pushing forward! We all do it at times, only to shake our heads later, at our bull-headedness. If we bet and hit a wall, we need to start sensing that there is a wall there, instead of trying to deny it or otherwise rationalize it away. When we feel something solid up ahead, stop trying to push on through. We cannot win at poker until we correctly perceive these signals.

When you see the enemy to be empty, proceed; where you see the enemy to be full, stop.

—Zhuge Liang

Feel the rhythm of the game. Thrust when strong, fall back when weak. Follow the example of the Japanese martial art of Aikido, in which a thrusting blow to one side results in the person rolling out of the way to the other.

Poker, like most other activities occurring at their highest levels, is a rhythm. They thrust, you parry; you thrust, they fall back. It is a rhythm that you join in and become attuned to.

If a player is not in a normal rhythm or in balance with the game, that is a signal that something is wrong. Good players spot this rhythm shift as quickly as a musician hears a note out of tune.

—Steve Fox, *Cardplayer* magazine

POKER RULE #44: Join the rhythm.

How do you join the rhythm? It is as simple as forging forward and pulling back.

Be attuned to who, and how many, of your opponents are betting (or not betting)—to the symbiotic ebb and flow, the strength of your hand within this flow, and the back-and-forth parrying that occurs in the game.

The Zen of poker is a rhythm located somewhere in the crossroads between playing loose at the wrong times and playing loose at the *right* times; between betting strongly, and alternately pulling back and withdrawing. It is a subtle intersection, and misjudged, it can still unravel, even today, even in expert hands, Zen or no Zen. It can zig when you zag.

Any miscue at this cosmic intersection can derail things on a given night.

♥ ♣ ♦ ♠

Such miscues generally result from not reading the situation correctly—for example seeing an opponent as weak, who is merely pretending to be weak; trying to push through a good hand in the face of clearly strong competition; failing to bet when you should have bet; not backing off when another player is very hot; not recognizing your own emotions getting out of control, and so on. It is generally a case of being out of harmony with what is going on.

"Out of harmony" is just what it sounds like—an individual who is bumping into desk corners, fighting with office copier machines, being belligerent with people, and being generally in conflict with his environment and out of sorts in a variety of ways. Such a person has ceased to be part of the flow, and to move with it. The same happens in poker.

POKER RULE #45: Observe the rhythm of the wall.

When your opponents are all betting away very strongly, smoothly, and confidently, the good cards are distributed *away from you*. Picture it as a wall, one that goes up on one side of the table and comes down on the other. Ask yourself where you are in relation to this. Don't take on the high wall with your low wall.

You may have noticed that at the times when you are running cold in a game the players across the table are cheerfully betting and raising, and oppositely, when you start getting good cards, there is a kind of collective downturn of fortunes across the table—a faltering, a hesitancy.

One reason for this is that the good cards in your hand are *not* in someone else's hand. When the wall of strength goes up on one side, it invariably starts to crumble on the other. Observing the rhythm of this back-and-forth movement of walls being constructed is taking a larger view of the game that has origins in Zen.

POKER RULE #46: Wait your turn.

This may sound too simple to be true, but maybe it is not far from the mark: let the other fellow have his victories, and at other times he will withdraw and let you have yours. (A player sometimes says, when folding: "I'm going to get out of your way.")

Wait until you have the better hand. This is when it is your turn. (This might not necessarily mean having a great hand; it might mean having an *average* hand when everyone else is weak.) Get yourself into this rhythm.

Be patient. Your turn will come. It will generally be dictated by the betting on various sides of the table. The lull is your turn. And have no doubt, your turn *will* come. Be ready when it does.

If you have a great hand, but there are three or four other players eagerly raising and reraising, the chances are that this is not your turn, even though you may have terrific cards. Conversely, you may have mediocre cards but sense weakness all around the table—and this *might* be your turn. Tune into this!

POKER RULE #47: Fit yourself into the flow of the game.

Some players approach the game of poker simply as a game, the way you might play Chinese checkers, or Old Maid. They can be observed playing their *own* cards and nothing else, staring hard at their hand, brows furrowed, never glancing up, struggling along. It's as if they are playing in a vacuum. Still others do the opposite, trying to dominate all parts of the game, force victory, muscle over the game with various aggressive maneuvers. We might say that the former group doesn't know there is a flow going on, while the latter group is trying to annihilate it, stamp it out. In Zen, the correct approach is always the middle way—neither passive nor trying overly hard to dominate.

Do either of the above two approaches work? Yes, intermittently. A better approach—one that experience shows works more frequently—is to try to fit yourself into the flow of it. Your chances of placing yourself *into* a game and winning by this means are generally better than your chances of both playing solitary *or* bulling your way over it and beating it.

The proof of this: How many times have you seen someone play solitarily and win? Seven or eight times? And how many times have you seen someone sit down at the game and start betting heavily and extravagantly and win? Fifteen or twenty times? And how many times have you seen a player who sits down quietly and simply seeks to fit himself into the flow of the game, win by doing *this*? Fifty? Sixty? One hundred?

Think of the game as a puzzle, and your goal is to fit yourself in as a puzzle piece. If you try to fit in the wrong place—or force yourself in—awkwardness and disaster result. But if you consider the game as a whole, and find the place you were meant to fit (without trying to force it), things often reach an effortless state.

[Some Olympic athletes] . . . allude to a "zone" or trancelike state where time seems to slow and things seem crystal clear . . . You will not be able to force your way into the zone, but when you relax and focus on perfecting every detail, the zone will find you.

—Steve Fox, *Cardplayer* magazine

Most events have their own rhythm. You can try imposing your own rhythm on them, but usually this succeeds only for a short time. Unless you are very powerful (or very good), you ought to seek to join into the situation and operate within its rules and terms instead of trying to change or dominate it.

In fact, we might say that virtually everything that happens successfully in life happens because something "fit in" with something else. From the way men and women relate to a new guy joining the cave family to a bird riding on the back of a hippo in Africa to a new product on the market. This is a very deep underlying principle. Don't try to ignore it or go outside of it. Fit yourself into the flow.

In poker this might mean staying within the strength of your hands, not overplaying them, backing off in the face of stiff competition, folding when too many players are in against you, raising yourself when others show weakness, and so on.

POKER RULE #48: Become aggressive within the openings that appear.

Watch a professional basketball team in action sometime. Notice the best players on the team, and how they play. Now watch the second-string players when they come in off the bench. Notice how, by contrast, these players often flail about trying to make something happen, arms akimbo, using much greater energy, but energy that is dispersed wildly in every direction, sometimes succeeding, sometimes not. Note how much more efficiently is the energy expended by the better players—projecting it deftly into openings they see between their opponents, and if none exist, remaining stationary or falling back. Their energy either projects itself into the openings or conserves itself. Use this as a model for employing energy into the openings of poker that occur. Bad cards come up for all your opponents and there is silence, indicating doubt and hesitation; or you notice an opponent is playing bad cards consistently; or a player reveals that he will fold a good hand whenever you raise him. These are all openings for you to enter.

There is one further lesson that needs to be noted about these openings. When you watch a great player such as Michael Jordan being guarded by another player, you see a fine-tuned sense of when his opponent has shifted too far in one direction . . . and then Jordan would go the other way.

You *be* Michael Jordan in the game of poker . . . move back and forth with opponents following you, shadowing you, and when they overcorrect in one direction or another, you go the other way aggressively and pour it on. This is simply attuning yourself to the Zen rhythm of the game.

The enemy advances, we retreat; the enemy camps, we harass; the enemy tires, we attack; the enemy retreats, we pursue.

—Mao Tse-tung

Bumper Cars and the Head Butting of Rams: The Art of Conflict Avoidance

Playing poker could be compared to driving the bumper cars at the county fair.

The goal is to steer around the other bumper cars. It is not to look for confrontational points and jump at them. Some players, however, persist in thinking the object is to bump heads. To have this goal is similar to seeing young rams on a mountaintop butting heads with horns. In the meantime, unseen and unnoticed, the wise old ram avoids this situation and detours around it. Later, when the two young rams are resting from the rigors of their fight, the wise old ram walks right through the territory they were fighting over with no effort at all. In Zen, this is *naturalness*—the ordinary way. And in poker, too, this head butting is not really the object. The object is to steer carefully around these situations.

You will often see players banging each other back and forth with bets in a game, going head to head. They are like the young rams. They think success means battling for the big glamour pots, competing for the favor of the crowd with dramatic eye-catching victories. If such players would focus instead on acquiring a few smaller pots, quietly, every hour, they would slowly move into the lead. This is the way of the old ram. He is not there to make a statement with his play; he is gradually building a bankroll instead.

For the true warrior, there is no warfare.

—Chogyam Trungpa, *Shambhala:*
The Sacred Path of the Warrior

Winning is not the basic goal behind martial arts training. The truth—although many people seem to forget it—is that most of the arts are designed to skillfully avoid win-lose situations, to avoid conflict altogether.

—Chuck Norris, *The Secret Power Within*

POKER RULE #49: Pick your times of confrontation.

Would you rather have good cards when other players have good cards, or when they are weak and vulnerable? This is a Zen question with regard to poker. The latter is usually better. This is the time you will gain the most by having a confrontation. It is better to use your strength at this time, rather than during the times of *their* strength.

There is a famous cautionary Zen quote that says: "When two tigers fight, one will be killed and the other will be seriously wounded."

What this means is: Why use strength against strength?

World-class poker players can sometimes be seen avoiding these types of situations, folding excellent hands rather than knocking heads with another great player who also has a great hand. Why be wounded or killed? Withdraw; conserve your energy for a better opportunity. Pick your spots—times of confrontation—carefully.

Good warriors prevail when it is easy to prevail.

—Sun Tzu

In war, when adversaries are orderly in their movements and are at their sharpest, it is not yet time to fight with them; it is best to fortify your position and wait. Watch for their energy to wane after being on alert for a long time; then rise and strike them.

—Liu Ji

POKER RULE #50: Adjust your game for how much competition you have in the hand.

Many players play their cards exactly the same way every time, independently of how many opponents they are up against or how strongly these opponents are betting. They play a pair of aces in Hold'em or Seven-Card Stud all the way to the end of the hand, whether they are up against one player or six, whether three opponents are eagerly raising them or none. We need to factor these variables in. Why join in to times when it is an unfavorable circumstance?

Plan before acting. Fight only when you know you can win.

—Zhuge Liang

11

The Wall of Cards: Cyclical Luck

Victory shifts from man to man.

—Homer, *The Iliad*

Luck in any card game is cyclical—it comes and goes in a mysterious fashion. Sometimes the cards run hot, sometimes cold. Many players give no weight to this at all as a factor in the game. But if such events are cyclical, perhaps we ought to take a hard look at this as a factor in the game. It must be of some significance that in some games no matter how well we play nothing works, while in others it hardly matters what we do because we can't do anything wrong. It is unlikely that an effect of such magnitude would have no meaning within our own purposes in the game.

Since poker involves so many borderline decisions, often occurring one after another, it doesn't hurt to ask yourself from time to time (when trying to make up your mind about which way to go in a hand): "How is my luck running?" Asking yourself this can be helpful in maximizing your good days and minimizing your bad days.

As noted, some players ignore this completely. They play each hand independently, regardless of how their luck is running. You see these players betting along nonchalantly, playing each hand by the book, despite being down a lot of money. They have not retreated, despite the negative flow of events.

It can't hurt to monitor one's luck and the general trend of it: how hot or cold you are is a legitimate factor in the decision-making process. This is not just a question of academic interest. It has a direct bearing on your fortunes. Use this tool to answer some of the borderline decisions you make in the game.

If your cards are below average, but you've been winning with anything and everything, you might want to play more hands. Conversely, if you've been getting fairly good hands, but you've lost with all of them, you might want to fold some of these.

A mistake in many areas of life, not just poker, is to struggle against the trend. A sight that is often seen in poker games is players desperately trying to make all their strategies and experience work when nothing is working. When such a situation as this occurs, approach even good cards with a wary eye. Call bets grudgingly; be reluctant to raise. Keep a lower profile. Some players will tell you, "Well, if it's good cards, then you have no choice—you have to play the hand." You don't. Not if nothing is working.

Monitor trends in your luck—but not excessively. Keep an eye on them, but don't become a slave to them.

POKER RULE #51: Learn to play up and down the ladder.

Don't just downscale your *bets* when you get cold, downscale the actual way you play the game. Back off *within* your method of play, alternately loosening up your game when things are going well and tightening back up when they are not.

Mathematicians tell us that each hand takes place independently of all others. This is good advice to ignore. If things are going badly, back off. You may be playing in a game closer to your bankroll than your opponents are (or the experts), and thus cannot afford to test out the theory. Don't go home from a cardroom with a horrendous loss just because you read somewhere that mathematically "every hand is independent of every other," so you just kept betting away, despite the fact that you were losing every hand, one after the other. For *your* purposes the hands weren't operating independently of each other.

Longtime, experienced card players believe in the *bunching* of luck. They have seen it. They have felt it. They know it is not a pipe dream or a mirage. Ignore this phenomenon at your peril. Even the mathematicians admit that it can happen, will happen, does happen, and has happened—they just dispute it when it *is* happening.

III

Nuts and Bolts

12

Include Failure in the System

However, though I don't want to die, I want to practice so that when I'm faced with death, I'll think nothing of it.

—Suzuki Shosan, *Warrior of Zen*

You are called samurai. Should you not be ready to die?

—Zen master Hakuin

Death in the game of poker is part of the process, and the game cannot be mastered without including it. This concept must be fully accepted by the player.

Those who are reluctant to give up their lives and embrace death are not true warriors.

—D. T. Suzuki, *Zen and Japanese Culture*

POKER RULE #52: Unlike many games and sports, poker has a third factor: the cards.

Imagine playing tennis if the ball had a mind of its own, if it could run off to the sidelines and bounce up and down for a minute or two. Imagine a game of golf where the ball could occasionally go off down the fairway, dance about, and do whatever it wanted. Imagine a chess game in which the pieces suddenly became worthless, or a hockey game in which the puck suddenly went against everything the players were trying to do.

With poker, this additional factor sometimes exists. And this makes it more than just a simple game—your skill versus your opponents' skill. The cards can go cold for you and hot for them, or start doing all manner of crazy things.

As a result, you never quite control poker. It is more like rodeo riding, where you try to keep the bull under you as much of the time as possible. It is a kind of shepherding of one's luck toward a given destination—something that is every bit as difficult as it sounds.

In fact, due to luck's part in the mix, there is sometimes a feeling that there is a point beyond which expertise cannot go, a point forever off-limits. Yet at the same time it is this challenge that attracts us and keeps us coming back.

Skill and Luck in Poker

It is sometimes difficult even for an expert player to fully grasp the concept of a game that requires a large degree of both skill *and* luck. The fact is, very few other sports or games in life work this way. Most competitions require either one or the other, not both.

What kind of game is it, the player may wonder, what kind of exquisite torture, that requires a person to be both highly skillful *and* lucky on a given day? What torturer of a medieval age dreamed up such a combination as this? (It's as if a football team were required not only to dominate its opponent on the field through sound, skillful play, but also to avoid, during the game, some third party shooting at it randomly from the sidelines.)

POKER RULE #53: Include Failure in the System.

Because of this random luck factor, it is possible for failure to raise its head at any moment. Consequently, we can't sidestep or ignore it; we have to find a place for it in our overall system.

This is more profound than it seems. Any Zen-like state attained on the part of the player must be flexible enough to adapt not only to changing events but also to the vagaries of chance and the harmony continued in spite of it.

To put it another way, no matter what Zen-like state the player is able to get himself into, he will still be at the mercy of Lady Luck. This outside element is uncontrollable and does not fall under Zen's influence.

The real underlying problem is that we can't "will" our harmony onto outside events. It might be possible to do so in some activity where you totally control all aspects of it, but not in one where some part of it is outside of your control. (Harmony that *is* achieved in situations where the person doesn't have total control—working at a job, for instance—is almost always a matter of fitting oneself into the existing system, and that is the case here.) Thus, calm and Zen-like as we may be, we can't change outside events, and as a result, "bad beats" and other untimely occurrences will continue to occur. However, while we can't will our harmony onto outside events, we can adopt a *higher* harmony that includes the bad occurrences under the larger umbrella of this harmony.

The game of poker as it unfolds from the player's perspective is experienced as an alternating of in harmony and out of harmony—things going right, things going wrong. Both of these must be bracketed together and contained underneath this *larger* harmony.

Adapting to random surprise wrenches thrown into your plans while still remaining in harmony is the challenge of poker.

Including failure in our poker strategy also has another Zen-like quality. It brings about humility. Factoring it into our game means realizing that while we may win 55 percent of the time, we will also lose the other 45 percent—working *with* this fact and accepting it, rather than fighting it. (If you could walk through a doorway and know that 55 percent of the time you would be treated like royalty, and 45 percent of the time you'd be beat up, would you walk through that door in a cocky, arrogant way?

Whenever we incorporate the possibility of failure into a system, humility appears.)

The mood, of course, may look cocky—you may even want it to look that way—but down deep it is not cocky. Humility is the Zen way (and probably the poker way as well).

Defeats in poker are not really defeats, anyway; they are more like trial balloons we keep sending up, knowing in advance that a certain number of them are going to get shot down.

Correctly played, therefore, poker is really a process of two steps forward and one step back.* The one-step-back part will always seem like a defeat, will always *feel* like a defeat, but it is not a defeat—simply part of the process.

Perhaps we must always advance a little by zig-zags.
—Theodore Roosevelt

Many players seem to have trouble understanding this concept. They cannot get their mind around it. Some are able to attain a composed, Zen-like calm and harmony when they are winning, but go berserk when losing. Others become defeatist when things turn bad. Still others become resigned or go on tilt in various ways. However, there is one other approach we would like to look at briefly, one other response to the negative turns of fortune that occur, and that is retreating to a *black-and-white game.*

This refers to players who seek to abolish losing completely from their game. This group is so adamantly opposed to losing that they try to do everything in their power to avoid it. The solution they choose is to tighten up their game to the nth degree. But unfortunately (as we have seen), swings in fortune are part of the game and need to be *included.* They must be worked with and controlled, not eliminated. (Don't worry. You are not *adapting* to failure by doing this, which is a different thing entirely.)

*There is some evidence that this two steps forward and one step back is more than just a figure of speech: pro players report that on average they expect to have two winning sessions out of every three.

This attempt to turn poker into a black-and-white game goes like this: "I'll play it absolutely safe. I will only stay on perfect hands, and if they are not perfect, then I'll drop out." On paper, this seems foolproof. The problem with this strategy is that you get trapped whenever you are in the gray areas (which is often). Poker is a dynamic, constantly changing game, with a lot of rough edges. Trying to be too perfect is like trying to keep your clothing and life vest perfectly arranged during a river-rafting trip. You must roll *with* the water as it is moving along, not try to confine and control it.

The life of Zen attainment is not like standing on a riverbank watching the current and appreciating the water or the landscape as a witness; it is jumping into the current and becoming one with it.

—Trevor Leggett, *A First Zen Reader*

Finally—if one more reason is needed—there is also the frustration aspect that occurs if you try to banish all losses from your game. Stress occurs whenever a loss happens—anger, despair, indignation, outrage. Every hand becomes a life-and-death matter. This is the result of telling yourself that you must never fail. By including losses in the system, however, we anticipate them and thereby remove all the power from them. We are cool and composed; calmly factor them in and move on.

He who fears being conquered is sure of defeat.

—Napoléon Bonaparte

The Probability Shotgun in Decision Making

Occasionally you will see a player triumph over you in a poker game, slamming his cards down victoriously, grinning smugly. You are the expert, his expression says, and look, I have just triumphed over you.

Such a display demonstrates that he does not understand very well the decision-making process that occurs in poker. For the truth is, losses occur. If the best player on earth—whomever that happens to be at this moment in time—is playing somewhere right now, he is losing hands. Not a lot, probably, but some. To treat him as if, being this good, he is never going to lose a hand is to show a misunderstanding of the game.

Certain situations arise over and over in which you use what is called a probability shotgun. It means nothing more than that conditions have become favorable for a win. It does not mean that you *will* win.

All business proceeds on beliefs or judgments of probabilities, and not on certainties.

—Businessman Charles Eliot

13

A Few Rules on Hesitating

No matter what you plan to do, act on the thought as it arises without deliberation.

—Suzuki Shosan

POKER RULE #54: All hesitations are noted.

The game of poker eventually reaches a certain rhythm in which, if you hesitate, it tells the other players something. For this reason it is necessary to know the game so well that you make decisions instantly and are able to control your hesitations—or lack thereof. And this means sufficient practice to retain this ability. If you play poker only a few times a year, this is one of the abilities you lose. Your hesitations become genuine.

Likewise, on the other side of the ledger, the hesitations of your opponents can provide valuable information. These hesitations can tell you where they are at in a hand—simply by eliminating one by one what they could have. (With certain hands, the player wouldn't hesitate at all. Or at certain *points* in the hand he wouldn't hesitate, if indeed he had a certain hand.)

Good poker players can *feel* hesitations. It's as though they sense electromagnetic changes in the air that signify doubt or fear or indecision. It's like a change in the ozone they pick up instinctively.

POKER RULE #55: Prolong the time spent looking at your cards.

Obvious, clear-cut, good cards lead to easy decisions. No player sits and stares at four kings minute after agonizing minute, trying to figure out what to do with them. But perhaps they should.

Vary how long you look at your cards. Your actions *are* being observed.

Hesitate at different times and at wrong times for the kind of hand you have. Hesitate for a while on cards you intend to fold. Or consider looking at your cards—both good and bad—for the same length of time.

Somebody checking for weakness around the table will be thrown off by someone who always hesitates in his reactions, good or bad.

All of which is simply another way of saying:

POKER RULE #56: Resist your first impulse.

You may notice (by observing yourself) that if you get a good hand you tend to reach for your chips a little quicker than at other times. It is never a bad idea to resist your first impulse in poker.

14

Stealth, Sneakiness, and Cunning

The fox knows much, but more he that catches him.
—Anonymous

Several well-known poker writers, David Sklansky among them, have noted the importance of operating on different levels: knowing what your opponent has, what he thinks you have, and what he thinks you think he has. As opponents get trickier and more deceptive, more of this sort of double- and triple-level thinking is called for.

Playing your hand straightforwardly, for instance, when you have an opponent who is assuming that you will be deceptive, or vice versa. Identifying which level you are currently at in this psychological battle becomes an art form against various opponents.

Conventional wisdom states that straightforward play is better against less-skilled opponents. Subtle, complex plays are wasted on them, because they are not really noticing.

To overcome the intelligent by folly is contrary to the natural order of things; to overcome the foolish by intelligence is in accord with the natural order. To overcome the intelligent by intelligence, however, is a matter of opportunity.
—Zhuge Liang

As your eyes scan the table during a betting round, beware of players who are sitting motionless as others shake their heads and

complain. Also beware of players shaking their heads and complaining.

———————

The rule is: When the enemy is far away but tries to promote
hostilities, he wants you to move forward.

—Sun Tzu

———————

Or, to put it another way, as Peter Høeg writes in his novel
Smilla's Sense of Snow:

If you're hunting shy animals, like reindeer, you let them
catch sight of you a few times on purpose. You stand up and
wave the butt of your rifle. In all living creatures, fear and
curiosity are closely related in the brain. The reindeer comes
closer. It knows that it's dangerous. But it has to come and
see what's moving like that.

Beware of players who are "waving the butt of their rifle."
Also beware of players who are simply calling all the way, seemingly reluctantly, as you continue to push forward and bet. (But
who are not dropping out.) This may very well be a case of "laying
in the weeds," passively playing an excellent hand before springing
the trap. Do not assume by this apparent weakness that all is well.

———————

Whenever you pursue people on the run, chasing beaten
soldiers, you must make sure whether they are really fleeing
or just feigning.

—Liu Ji

———————

POKER RULE #57: Be flexible.

Be a little unpredictable. If you do everything exactly the same
way every time, your opponents soon calibrate that to your betting and your cards.

Make it harder for opponents to see a pattern. Alternate raising with slow playing (playing a good hand very quietly). Throw in hesitations and wrong bets occasionally, but don't overdo it. Occasionally make a wrong play. Randomize your play. Don't fall into a predictable pattern.

Whoever has form can be defined, and whoever can be defined can be overcome.

—Sun Tzu II, *The Lost Art of War*

Zen, as a spiritual discipline . . . is consistently opposed to rigidity . . . Fixity is death; fluidity is life.

—Winston L. King, *Zen and the Way of the Sword*

Be unpredictable.

Induce others to construct a formation while you yourself are formless.

—Sun Tzu, *The Art of War*

Be flexible, but don't get *too* carried away with it. In short:

POKER RULE #58: Don't out-clever yourself.

Stick to basic poker most of the time. Keep the creativity (deliberately wrong plays) to a minimum. The temptation—especially when playing against longtime friends, where insults, dares, and egos are the norm—is to try to be cute, to do a double or triple-reverse on somebody, to give the boys something to talk about; opening with the wrong cards say, hoping for a miracle fill on later cards . . . and so on. The problem with this sort of thing is that it only works, statistically, about one or two times in ten. All such attempts as this get away from basic poker. They begin to drift into the area of long odds. Be unpredictable—but don't outclever yourself.

Finally, a positive attitude is helpful. Don't fall into the trap of becoming paranoid, and seeing unbeatable hands (of opponents) around every corner and behind every tree. Never forget that you're not the only one who has problems. Your opponents have problems, too. Play into *their* worst imaginings—don't be afraid to use their problems as part of your strategy.

In war one sees one's own difficulties, and does not take into account those of the enemy; one must have confidence in oneself.

—Napoléon Bonaparte

15

The Poker Face and Body Language

The power of expression resides in gestures of the most sparing kind.
—Eugen Herrigel, *The Method of Zen*

Zen teaches the greatest economy of expression and action.
—Neville Shulman, *Zen in the Art of Climbing Mountains*

POKER RULE #59: Perfect the poker face.

Most top poker players don't react much to events around them. A bomb could go off at the next table and they probably wouldn't react at all. The reason for this is that sometimes during the game a bomb *does* go off (a horrific card pops up) and how you react to this fact can cost you a lot of money. Because other players are *looking* for a reaction—or lack of reaction. It is best to always look as though no card that appears has any effect on you whatsoever; either that, or that every card that appears is exactly the card you knew and expected to appear.

It is all right to allow your eyes to express your will but never let them reveal your mind.
—Winston L. King, *Zen and the Way of the Sword*

POKER RULE #60: Determine whether an opponent is acting.

In a general way, assign each of your opponents a deceptiveness rating. If Player A across the table develops a downcast look during a hand and then turns over a very *good* hand, make a mental note of it. If Player B, next to him, does the same thing, and then turns over a *losing* hand, make a note of this, too. Player B was reacting honestly to his hand. Player A was acting. Which of these two people is capable of deceptiveness later on in the game? It is helpful to categorize each player because at some time you will likely bump into each of them heads-up in a hand, and into the same expressions.

Watch how players act when they are in big pots and there is a lot of money on the line. How nervous are they? Are they completely calm and composed? If a key card comes up that could affect their hand, do they even blink, flinch, or react? Some players don't. These are the players who have had more experience and are capable of deceptive plays when you are in against them. They have just rated their experience level for you.

In general, most good players don't do a great amount of acting because: they don't want to get caught at it, this tells their opponents something if they do get caught at it, it only works once if they get caught at it, and (most important of all) it is simply too much trouble—it is much easier, and saves a lot of energy, to have no expression at all than it is to do a lot of "acting."

The "right" face for Fighting Back is probably the blankest face . . . [Keep] the expression as neutral—but powerful—as possible."

—*Aikido in Everyday Life*

POKER RULE #61: Learn to read your opponents' voices.

Don't forget to listen to players' voices, too, and *act* on what you hear there. If a certain smooth, easygoing confidence enters an opponent's voice, this is usually a sign for you to be wary (or fold). Most players have a sliding scale of certainty in their tone of voice, as well as their other actions, that matches their hand—or at least what they *think* of their hand. This certainty is usually part of a package—voice, gestures, facial expression, calmness, coolness, composure, and so on. You *must* go by this, unless you feel it is an act.

I consider it to be the embodiment of swordsmanship to perceive the signs which occur before an opponent's actual movements.

—Munenori, a Tokugawa shogunal instructor quoted in *Zen and the Way of the Sword*

IV

Warrior Zen

16

Betting

What discourages opponents from coming is the prospect of harm.

—Sun Tzu

POKER RULE #62: Good poker is not a gentleman's game, it is a war.

This sounds like the dustiest of clichés, but it is true. It doesn't mean that everyone in the game has to be rude, or a jerk, never cracking a smile, but it means that aggressiveness is part of the game and is essential in gaining certain strategic advantages at different points in the game. For this reason, when played correctly, it does not fall within the polite, tea-party range.

This level is not reached immediately. Friendly games can go on for years or decades quite passively. Hardly any of the players bet (they all "check" around the table), and when someone does bet, no one ever raises—a polite, sociable version of "showdown" (that is, just turning the cards over at the end to see who wins).

Beyond this point, however, a different dynamic begins to reveal itself. Once everyone at the table begins betting their hands (instead of just calling) and using other means to maximize their play, poker leaves the realm of the polite game and at that point is probably being played as it should be. It becomes a game in which you pick your spots, attack, and retreat strategically.

POKER RULE #63: You're never going to win at poker by calling.

Calling bets (but never raising) is not the road to success in poker. Checking and calling do not take advantage of strategically favorable situations that occur. While it is true that the player who uses this approach will find himself winning from time to time, he will usually be seen winning on one occasion and losing the next. When he has the upper hand in a game, he doesn't use it. He doesn't bet or raise to get more money in the pot, bluff, get a free card, or thin the field by knocking out other players behind him, who then have a chance to keep playing and outdraw him. Good poker hands are like a powerful lever that can be used to move a large boulder, but it is left unused.

In the movie *Rounders*, a young professional poker player named Mike McDermott (played by Matt Damon) watches an amateur game between lawyers and judges in which everyone is checking all the way through the hand and no one is betting on their cards. In frustration, he seizes the chips of his friend in the game, a law school dean, and begins throwing them in for him, betting on the other man's hand. The point of the scene is the need for aggression when you have a good hand—not inertia and passivity.

Most important thing . . . is premium hands . . . If a bet's good enough to call, you're in there raising. Tight but aggressive.

—Kevin Canty, from *Rounders*

There is no working middle course in wartime.

—Winston Churchill

POKER RULE #64: Minimize your losses; maximize your gains.

The majority of players could significantly improve their game by folding more often when they have bad cards and betting more when they have good cards.

Oddly enough, players often tend to do the opposite. When they have a mediocre hand they stay in (instead of folding), and when they have a good hand they timidly check or bet the minimum.

For some unknown reason, in this (as well as other areas of life), the average person is not accustomed to betting a lot when things turn favorable. He is not used to upping the stakes at these times. He is used to betting the minimum amount when things turn favorable. He becomes tentative, skeptical, fearful. Perhaps he is so relieved to *have* a winning situation that he just sits back and accepts the win. But the problem here, again, is that by doing this, over the long run your win sizes tend to equal your loss sizes. (A good deal of the actual money winning takes place in the *difference* between win sizes over loss sizes over time—losing $50 on the times you lose, on average, say, while winning $100 on average when you win.)

He who soars not suffers no fall.

—Zen proverb

POKER RULE #65: Play tight and defensively until you have something—then bet a lot.

This is a popular technique—because it works. Its greatest weakness, perhaps, is its predictability—(since it is so straightforward, other players begin to notice the pattern that emerges, and adjust their play)— and its second greatest weakness is the player forgetting about it and abandoning it later on in the heat of battle. For it to work, you have to keep doing it, not get swept up in the action and let it slip from mind.

———————

In battle, momentum means riding on the force of the tide of events. If enemies are on the way to destruction, then you follow up and press them.

—Liu Ji

———————

Expert players also use this technique, of course, with the added capacity to mix it up and switch gears and randomize their game, as well as an ability to proceed intuitively, based on a balance of incoming signals and probabilities. They proceed on a *feel*—an instinctive reading of the game based on this congregate of signals. The less advanced player ought to stick closer to the notion, however, of waiting until a feeling of great certainty has been reached before playing—but of making sure he *does* play when he has the cards—and bets on them!

———————

Make sure you're right, then go ahead.

—Davy Crockett

———————

The good fighters of old first put themselves beyond the possibility of defeat, and then waited for an opportunity of defeating the enemy.

—Sun Tzu, *The Art of War*

———————

Here is another illustration of this same idea and why it is so important. Let's pose the following hypothetical question: Would it be fair to the other players in the game if everybody had to put in $40 or $50 whenever *you* had good cards, but only had to put in $5 or $10 when *they* had good cards?

The answer would be no, it wouldn't be fair at all. It would give you a big advantage in the game.

Therefore, this is the situation, through betting, that you try to get to. When you have the good cards, build the pot; when you have marginal cards, play passively and try to keep the betting down.

Bet heaviest at the *strongest* times.

POKER RULE #66: Learn how to bet extravagantly and wildly at times yet be able to turn it off completely at others.

This is a tricky transition to make, and many players never master it. As a result, many of them settle on a compromise: playing either one way or the other *all* the time—either wild and reckless, or tight and predictable. Many of the legendary bettors fail over the long run because they can't turn it off. And it is difficult to bet lavishly and freely at the right times, yet retreat into monklike quietude at other times. This is achieved by self-discipline and being flexible, not locking your game into one or the other extreme.

The warrior meditates only when he is performing his duty. As soon as he puts aside his sword, he relaxes his attention.
                                        —Suzuki Shosan, *Warrior of Zen*

POKER RULE #67: Learn the language of betting.

In betting, you're asking your opponent what he has, and he's telling you (more or less). It's a primitive language, like Indian smoke signals or car horns on the freeway—a form of tribal grunts with each side (hopefully) understanding the message and intent of the other.

Use betting as a probe, to ask for reactions (and don't forget to *watch* for reactions when you do this). If an opponent has a better hand than you, he will generally let you know.

Whenever you move against anyone, before mobilizing the army first use spies to see whether the opponents are many or few, empty or full, active or quiet. Then you can be very successful and never fail to win in battle.

—Liu Ji

POKER RULE #68: Higher betting levels often induce a new emotional range on players' faces.

Not everyone is used to increased betting levels. Tight players especially get thrown off by this. Strain appears; anxiety, hesitations. When the betting goes to the next level—especially if several players aren't used to it—it helps you read reactions. A new emotional range is revealed. It is the difference between telling someone their car has been scratched versus telling them their house has burned down. Get people on emotional ground they are not accustomed to and new information is often forthcoming. At lower betting levels they are all quite comfortable and easily hide their reactions. At higher levels, reactions begin to appear— in the form of doubts, uncertainties, and furrowed brows.

Here is an example: How readable would you be in a poker game at $1 a card? Now how readable would you be at a $1,000 a card? To an opponent who was used to playing for $1,000 a card, someone who did it every day, your reactions would probably be an open book. You would have some serious misgivings at each step along the way that he would be quite used to watching for. Players always watch other players' faces in poker, but they often become billboards once serious money is on the line.

POKER RULE #69: All other things being equal, big money can run you out of a game.

Many $5–$10 players sometimes move up to the $10-$20 level and the $10–$20 players sometimes move up to the $20-$40 level, and so on. At the next level above them, they are usually swimming with the sharks and looking at what is to them big money.

For reasons cited above, big money can reveal your stress points in a game, your hesitations and doubts, and pour it on unmercifully with raises and re-raises to disrupt your game. By this means, opponents gradually tip the scales in their favor. Moral: Don't be under-funded, and don't play in games that are out of your financial range.

POKER RULE #70: Get out when everything is going against you.

Beware of the situation that sometimes occurs in which you find yourself falling behind on *all* fronts: your bankroll is low, you don't have the resources of your opponents, your chip pile is shrinking, you are getting slightly worse cards than your opponents, your luck is slightly off its mark, and you are also being outplayed, because your opponents are using all of the above against you in *combination* to gradually wear you down. In addition, you may be responding to this situation by retreating into an extremely tight, defensive posture, something that becomes progressively self-strangling, as well as easy to read by the other players. This is a good time to get out.

17

Aggression

There is some risk of equating the entire foregoing discussion (of the Zen-like state) with passivity. While the two may appear similar, they are not the same thing.

Aggression exists in nature. What may look like a harmless bumble bee is a highly aggressive force on its own level, engaged in a life-and-death battle. What appears to be a delicate flower is in fact an organism violently struggling and forcing itself into life. These and other delicacies (at least as they appear to the human eye) could easily be mistaken for some form of passivity, when in fact there is a very different paradigm present.

In poker, too, there is another reality that exists, one that takes place above and beyond, in another sphere. This book would be incomplete if it were not mentioned. (It was touched on briefly in the previous chapter.) For lack of a better term, let's call this sphere Maximum Aggression. It is an utterly fearless Zen that happens in more advanced play, and usually appears in some hard-to-miss form such as persistent chip-firing combativeness. And indeed, at this next level of play, aggressiveness often rules.

Withdraw like a mountain in movement, advance like a rain-storm. Strike and crush with shattering force; go into battle like a tiger.

—Zhuge Liang

The nature of such aggressiveness is forceful, ruthless, and un-merciful. It is the Mack truck of strategy, the sledgehammer of methodology, the bulldozer of technique. Yet because of this it has a built-in danger that is always ever present: overplaying (a condition that risks departing from the Zen-like flow of the game, as discussed earlier).

Such super-aggression is not seen very often at lower levels of play or in friendly home games.

Let's define this aggression.

First, we don't mean betting when you have a good hand; this is normal and natural. Every poker player knows this. (Okay, al-most every one.) We mean continued raising and re-raising to the absolute maximum at every available opportunity.

He who is skilled in attack flashes forth from the topmost heights of heaven, making it impossible for the enemy to guard against him.

—Sun Tzu, *The Art of War*

What is the reasoning behind this type of play? Put in every-day language, it is the idea of dominating the game, taking con-trol, forcing opponents to play your game (rather than the opposite), forcing them into mistakes and decisions they'd rather not make. The idea is to be *pro*-active rather than reactive. Don't react to others, is the theory; take the initiative. A second impor-tant goal is forcing the weaker players out before they "hang around,"—keep playing and accidentally hit something, making it far too expensive for them too continue. This style of play is often chosen by players who have become tired of getting run down by bad players with bad cards who shouldn't even be in the hand. Consequently, when the aggressive player has good cards and takes them to the end of the hand, they win a high percentage of the time because, due to his previous aggressive betting, the other players with the bad hands are no longer around.

In battle, if the adversary is the defender and you are the invader, just try to penetrate deeply into their territory. If you penetrate deeply into their territory, defenders cannot win.
—Liu Ji

If you find yourself encountering real-life black-suited shadow warriors, remember the words of Sun Tzu: "Go to meet those who attack first. Waiting is bad? . . . Observe their attacking order, and go to meet those who attack first."
—Chuck Norris, *The Secret Power Within*

Players who employ this super-aggressive technique would argue that you *must* raise and re-raise in order to give yourself the best chance to win. They would say that it isn't an option. It results in less players in the hand at the end who have a chance to outdraw you.

And there is a large grain of truth to this. Players who hit a bad *flop* (the community cards in the middle of the table in Hold'em or Omaha) are often players who shouldn't be in. They are players the better players should have raised and re-raised until they were out. And from your own point of view, if we take these players out of the picture, a lot of times you're back in it again, even with a hand that turns weak at the end.

As an example, in Omaha high-low, if you and I both have an Ace-Ace-2-3 (an excellent hand), and another player has a 3-10-10-King off-suit (a terrible hand), and we don't raise, and a 10 comes on the next card and this other player wins with three 10's, its our own fault that we lost. We should have raised him out.

The underlying principle: When the flop comes bad, it hits the bad player.

It doesn't hit all the bad players, but it hits one of them. A second example: A player enters a pot in Hold'em with an 8-4 off-suit (a terrible hand) and the flop *also* comes bad, 8-4-2. Now he has two pair. It is the bad *player* who hits the bad *flop*.

The question for the good players is this: Why is this other player still in? Why didn't you raise him out?

At any rate, this is some of the reasoning behind super-aggressive play.

While it will certainly *feel* more expensive to play like this—to be constantly, aggressively throwing in chips, constantly raising—the fact is, whenever we allow an extra one or two players in a hand, one of them invariably outdraws us and ends up *costing* us money in the long run.

Still, such aggressive play must always be tempered with a measure of caution and common sense. We are not talking about just blind blasting of bets into the pot without reason. The danger, always, is overplaying—a trap even good players sometimes fall into. The dangers of this kind of forceful aggressiveness are summed up nicely in the following quote about aikido.

That's the nice thing about sincere, focused attacks: They are so clearly directed . . . so committed to destroying you that they develop their own momentum and energy. That momentum will carry them past you if you . . . turn at the right moment.

—Terry Dobson and Victor Miller, *Aikido in Everyday Life*

Final Note

The style of play described above as super-aggressive is dangerous territory for the average player. It will result in much greater fluctuation in his bankroll. While he ought to know this realm exists—and perhaps even experiment with it from time to time—he is probably better off sticking with the style of play he feels comfortable with.

Indeed, it is not only difficult to play like this (at this level), it is also difficult to keep at it. To continue it indefinitely, unemotionally, and without faltering or ever backing off—often in the face of repeated adversity—takes a special relentlessness of purpose not found in many players.

18

Warrior Zen

The samurai were professional warriors, men trained to fight and die, so it was only natural that they were drawn to a philosophy that offered detachment from the physical world, a way of conquering the self so thoroughly and absolutely that death could be faced without fear.
—Chuck Norris, *The Secret Power Within*

The samurai were a class of feudal warriors who emerged in sixteenth- and seventeenth-century Japan. Power had shifted throughout Japan from the larger regimes and dynasties of earlier centuries to smaller, more fragmented regional entities. These smaller entities were headed by a series of feudal warlords who built castles and supported neighboring towns. The class structure of the time began to operate around these clans and feudal barons, and a professional class of warrior-knights arose to defend them. In time, the samurai became a powerful ruling class of its own, reaching its peak in the Tokugawa dynasty.

The samurai adopted their own version of Buddhism, which came to be known as Warrior Zen (or Samurai Zen). It is the application of Zen to warfare.

Yet the notion itself brings up a question.

The sword is generally associated with killing, and most of us wonder how it can come into connection with Zen, which is a school of Buddhism teaching the gospel of love and mercy.

—D. T. Suzuki, quoted in *Zen and the Way of the Sword*

Why Zen for those whose specialty is combat? How can Zen be employed for warlike situations? Or (to take the case of poker) how to apply Zen-like ideas of harmony to a game whose essence is aggression and confrontation? The answer is significant for the poker player. It is found in the area of detachment and centeredness.

In actual combat, [the pupil's] mind must be calm and not at all disturbed. He must feel as if nothing critical is happening . . . His behavior is not in any way different from his everyday behavior. No change is taking place in his expression. Nothing betrays the fact that he is now engaged in a mortal fight.

—Masahiro Adachi, *Zen and Japanese Culture*

For the samurai, the application of Zen was used as a calming influence to center himself before battle, thereby allowing the perfection of the mechanics of aggression.

Of what use was a sharp, well-balanced long sword, or an intricate and technically elaborate method of using it in combat, if the warrior . . . had not developed a stable, inner platform of mental control from which to act or react according to the circumstances of an encounter?

—Osar Ratti and Adele Westbrook,
The Secrets of the Samurai

POKER RULE #71: Know your game so well that you can act without thinking.

Warrior Zen seeks to create, ultimately, a kind of faultless expertise—one so automatic that it can function by second nature, without conscious thought. How is this possible? How can we function without thinking about it in a poker game? Don't we need to think at every point?

The answer is: It is like playing music, or typing on a computer or typewriter. Do we consciously stop and think at every note we play or every letter we type? Or does the brain forge on past this because the technique has become so deeply ingrained in us that we do it automatically? (We sometimes see this illustrated in movies by the character of a sword-wielding samurai who is wearing a blindfold—he must proceed solely by feel and nothing else.)

No matter what the activity—be it music, art, sports, a profession or trade—there is a state of achievement wherein it becomes so perfected through practice and a certain mental attitude, that it seems to function independently of the performer.

—Arthur Sokoloff

Practically speaking, there are a lot of situations in poker you don't *want* to think too long and hard about. You want, if possible, to react instinctively, *within* the rhythm. If you think too long, you can outthink yourself and get off the rhythm (as well as tip off opponents to your hand; "paralysis by analysis" this has been called). You want, if possible, to get where you can proceed on an automatic "sense" that has become built-in, through years of experience.

The master musician in concert . . . becomes "mindless," that is, totally beyond the conscious thought of what notes to play, what fingers to use, or how vigorously or softly to deal with the successive notes. All these things have long since become ingrained in mind and muscle. The music becomes a living thing flowing out of the blended unity of mind and muscle.

—Winston L. King, *Zen and the Way of the Sword*

This is the result of longtime practice—practice so exhaustive and thorough that all movements have become like involuntary reflexes.

A sense of effortlessness in performance reveals the mastery of one who has become one with his or her work . . . . The flow of Itzhak Perlman's violin music is in this sense not much different from Chris Evert's tennis game. The years of practice have flowered to a stage where it all just occurs.

—Arthur Sokoloff

In other words, reactions have reached such a state of second-nature that, in Eugen Herrigel's phrase, "It is as if the sword wielded itself."

He leaves aside all conscious thoughts of proper methods, strategies, and tricks he will use. He will simply, unconcernedly, "mindlessly," or No-Mindfully advance and strike when his deepest, uncalculating self dictates, when it takes over the management of his sword.

—Winston L. King, *Zen and the Way of the Sword*

Similarly, in poker, the goal is to be able to make decisions instinctively, with techniques able to respond automatically to every situation.*

---

*A study of chess grandmasters once revealed that they don't think ten or fifteen moves ahead (as we might think), but rather instinctively grasp the possibilities by an *intuitive* glance at the board.

In this manner, with chips close at hand, the experienced player is able to evaluate many incoming signals at once. His thought processes, steeped in countless hours of play, evaluate the likelihood of success, facial expressions of opponents, body language, the kind of hands they are likely to be playing, the probability of making his own hand, the size of the pot, his position in the betting order, and numerous other factors, and he reaches out seamlessly and makes the correct response—all the while carrying on a conversation with the player next to him.

19

Playing on Instinct

POKER RULE #72: As you become a more experienced poker player, try turning your game over to your instinct.

The most important part of the above sentence is the first part: as you become more experienced. Do this too early in your poker career and it may backfire, usually with disastrous consequences. But a point will come in your game when you'll feel more comfortable trusting your instincts. A feeling of confidence will occur regarding your abilities, your grasp of specific game situations and probabilities.

Once poker expertise has reached this level, playing by instinct becomes more attainable. Indeed, some players believe in playing the *vibes*—feeling their way almost intuitively. This usually takes many years at the table to achieve. But the good news is, if you make yourself play like this, you get better at it. And this is what many of the greatest players do.

Listen to your hunches, therefore, and your gut feelings. If something in your gut tells you to do something—or to *not* do something—during the game, pay attention to it. Give it a fair hearing. It may not be a hunch; more likely it is a collection of invisible signals pointing in a certain direction. (Many times you will hear players say, "I *knew* I was beat," but they don't act on this feeling.) Just because you're not conscious of where these hunches are coming from doesn't mean they aren't valid. In a sense, expertise is being able to raise these hunches to the conscious level and analyze them.

POKER RULE #73: Get to the point where you "put someone on a hand" and proceed on that assumption, then take the penalties that accrue from being wrong and the profits that accrue from being right.

In poker, to *put someone on a hand* means you predict specifically what hand they are playing and act according to this. This is done by watching various factors: how much they bet, *when* they bet, when they *stopped* betting, their hesitations, and the sort of hands they've been playing before. An example might be: if a possible flush comes on the board (the community cards in the middle of the table in Hold'em, or Omaha; also called the flop) and they bet, and then a pair comes, making a possible full house, and they stop betting—they probably have the flush. Or in Seven-Card Stud, if they have a king up and are betting, and an ace appears in another player's hand and they stop betting, they probably have a pair of kings.

Putting a player on a hand is a valuable skill, but due to the very specificness of the prediction, you can be wrong at times and it can occasionally blow up in your face. If practiced diligently, however, the profits that accrue from the times you are right will begin to outweigh the times when you are wrong and encourage you to proceed further down this path.

POKER RULE #74: Try playing on instinct.

As an exercise, try turning off your thinking mechanism from time to time and going by your instincts alone. (Cautionary note: As mentioned, this should not be tried until poker expertise has reached a certain level. You will know when you have reached this level, and in fact may have already begun to do this.)

At certain times in the game, proceed on instinct, on the feeling of the situation you're in. Are you in the lead in the hand? Do you sense that you have the edge and the momentum? (And here we come to another important point: if the answer is no, don't hesitate to go by *this* feeling, too. Players often fall into this trap. They are quite good at playing on instinct when they perceive the answer to be yes, that an opponent is weak, but turn a deaf ear to the other answer. They hear the little voice clearly when it says he is weak, but ignore it when it says he is strong. Hope, greed, and stubbornness come into play, and we rebel against the answer we're hearing. In fact, the answer will be no a greater portion of the time, simply because there are more of them than there are of us.)

Playing by instinct is going to be wrong at times but doing it on a regular basis will purify the process. From practice, you will close the gap. Your instinct will improve, until what is in your mind will gradually come into alignment with the true nature of what is going on in the game.

As noted, you will be wrong at times doing this. But if you keep at it, and don't let wrong guesses deter you from your course, eventually you're *not* going to be wrong quite as often. Most longtime players arrive at this point eventually, of course; but they get there by a very haphazard route, over years of play. Doing this deliberately speeds up the learning curve.

POKER RULE #75: Play on your second set of emotions, not your first.

What do we mean by second set? Your hunches, your intuition, your gut feeling of where you are at in a hand, your feel for the situation. Oddly enough, most players seem to have no qualms whatever about pushing in all their chips on their *first* set of emotions—(anger, greed, pride, ego, stubbornness, revenge, one-upmanship)—but they hesitate to do so on their second set of emotions! And these are often more accurate!

Playing on Instinct: A Caution

Playing on instinct requires regular play. Without regular, systematic practice, you may find yourself in deep water. Indeed, if you play on an irregular basis (or periodically take large amounts of time away from the game), and then try to play like this, you may find your skills too rusty to do so. You are in danger of misinterpreting signals and losing badly.

In fact, even with regular play, playing on instinct is still far from foolproof. It is based on intuition, an instinctual analysis of incoming signals, and is a very subtle effect. Animals of prey proceed this way. Tigers. And leopards. And great artists. And great athletes. And world-class experts in various fields. And occasionally . . . they guess wrong.

The tiger, for instance, with all the genetic hard-wired intuition of a thousand generations, with all his breeding, occasionally guesses wrong. Ten thousand years of heredity and instinct turn the wrong corner at the wrong time and come face to face with the wrong enemy. Instinct can be an invaluable tool. It can cut to the heart of the matter faster than logic, deduction, or other forms of analytical thought. But it can make mistakes, too, even at the very highest levels. It will never be 100 percent foolproof.

20

Consciousness

At the final table in the $2,000 Hold-'em event in 1997 at the World Series of Poker, poker pro Dan Heimiller wore a T-shirt with lettering on the front that said: "I DO WHATEVER THE VOICE IN MY HEAD TELLS ME TO DO."

Recent studies of the brain and human consciousness (as reported in Danish scientist Tør Nørretranders's book *The User Illusion*) suggest that the conscious mind is really only the tip of the iceberg of what we know, that we actually possess much more knowledge than we are consciously aware of.

A paragraph from the dust jacket of the book sums up the idea briefly:

> During any given second, we consciously process only sixteen of the eleven million bits of information our senses pass on to our brains. In other words, the conscious part of us receives much less information than the unconscious part of us. We should trust our hunches and pursue our intuitions because they are closer to reality than the perceived reality of consciousness.

This suggests that people are aware of much more that is going on than their conscious self realizes. (This also corresponds to Buddhism's doctrine that the mind is narrow and limited—only a part, not the whole of the person, which is what we should be applying to each moment.) The lesson for poker is that we ought to try to tap into this "other knowing," if possible. The way to do this is to first realize that it exists, and second, to remain clear-headed enough to be receptive to it. A final point is that we have to have the courage to *act* on it, too—to be able to "pull the trigger" (bet on our hunches).

If this knowledge is there and available but we are not receiving the signal, it is of no use. If it is available and we *are* receiving the signal but not acting on it, it is likewise of no use. It is like driving a car: if we sense a pothole upcoming in the road ahead and aren't receptive to this inner voice telling us about it, it does no good; if we do become aware of the pothole in the road up ahead but don't act on it and run over it anyway, it also does no good. (The little voice is often just below awareness, and this is the reason we don't act on it.)

Occasionally we get a glimpse, in our daily lives, of this "underground" store of knowledge we possess that is generally going unused. We may catch ourselves humming every note to a thirty-year-old song while busily engaged in some other task, unaware we're even doing it. Or we find ourselves carrying on one conversation while listening to another nearby at the same time. A telephone number barely glanced at during the middle of a conversation, we dial almost unthinkingly a moment later, and so on. These are indicators of greater knowledge existing under the surface. (Every few years a study comes out telling us this, that we only use some tiny percentage of our brain's potential.) Much of this knowledge that exists below the surface comes in the form of nonverbal clues and behaviors, which is certainly of interest to poker players.

As a practical matter, it is obviously impossible to possess *all* our knowledge at any one time. It is no different than trying to show all TV shows on a single TV screen at one time, or having an encyclopedia scattered around on the floor, open to every page. It is simply too cumbersome. We can't keep everything we know in the forefront of consciousness. But if there is a vast reservoir of knowledge existing under the surface, we need to tap into it or at least be receptive to the possibility of it. If we can access it in any way, through hunches or intuition, we ought to do so. As alluded to in Dan Heimiller's T-shirt slogan: we ought to listen to the "voice in our head."

One thing is for sure about this capability: we will not hear this voice if we are not listening for it.

21

Focus

Become more acutely aware of what's happening right now, this very moment.
—Phil Jackson, *Sacred Hoops*

One of the central aspects of Zen Buddhism is being present *in the moment*. When Buddhism speaks of being "awakened," this is what it refers to—the here and now, direct experience of daily life in each moment. Consequently, when turning over any aspect of your life to your instincts, poker or anything else, you must always take pains to make sure you are *grounded*—awareness (paying attention) must always be present. If this is absent then instinct, powerful as it is, begins to drift off into the netherworld, its feet no longer in contact with the ground, and you will find yourself disconnected from the task at hand.

The reason for this is simple: being in Zen-like synch with an activity and absentmindedly drifting are not that far apart. They share a dreamlike quality that, if not kept strictly in control, begins to stray from the path. It is for this reason that being in Zen-like harmony is not enough by itself. You still have to make sure you are paying attention—that is, operating in the moment.

This is a point Phil Jackson, former coach of the Chicago Bulls, emphasizes in his Zen/basketball book *Sacred Hoops*: "The point is to perform every activity, from playing basketball to taking out the garbage, with precise attention, moment by moment."

In other words, take your eye off the ball, and all the synchronicity of flow, skill, and past experience won't matter. You have to stay focused on the task at hand.

This can be illustrated quite simply by using a couple of everyday examples—driving a car, say, or tying our shoelaces—activities we are so good at doing (because we've done them thousands of times) that we can do them by second nature. If we let our mind drift while we are doing them, what happens? We may suddenly jerk awake to notice that we almost caused an accident with our car, or we may find, tying our shoelaces, that we now have to start over and tie them a second time. These are examples of what happens if we give over a task completely to our instinct. We will have to pay attention, no matter how much experience we've had at a thing or how many times we've done it before. If not, we still stray across the center line, like a sleepy driver crossing into the other lane. Instinct is dazzling—it can cut through thickets of knowledge and go right to the heart of a matter—but it is not sufficient in itself. Focus is its right arm. It can't operate without it.

Phil Jackson says: "Do each action with a conscious effort" and be "fully engaged in what you are doing." In short, part of the Zen of poker is to be fully present in the moment while we are playing. This is born out by top players, who are often described as "really having the ability to concentrate."

V

Emotions and
Opponents

22

Respect for Opponents

Destroyed people make bad enemies.
　　　　　　　—Terry Dobson and Victor Miller,
　　　　　　　　Aikido in Everyday Life

If you seek vengeance, dig two graves.
　　　　　　　　　　　　　　　—Proverb

Becoming Part of the Interlocking Whole

We saw the importance earlier of inserting ourselves into the rhythm of the game. This is true in a social sense, too. If you show respect for the other players in the game, they are likely to see you as a player who is playing at the next level, not one who is merely (and greedily, blindly) mired in his own self-interest.

They are more likely to respect your play and avoid taking mean-spirited and underhanded (and unpredictable) measures.

This does not mean they will lay off when playing against you or play less hard, it simply means fairness, consideration, and straightforward play. It means stability and harmony. You will respect your fellow players, and they in turn will respect you.

These things are all to your advantage.

(Observe the relationship between long-term poker players when they run into each other, and the respect that passes between them. They meet each other with a knowing twinkle in their eye, a camaraderie that wordlessly expresses all the past wars they've been through together. Mutual respect underlies it all.)

The restoration of harmony is the goal of all conflict.
—Terry Dobson and Victor Miller, *Aikido in Everyday Life*

Mutual respect is a predictable thing. It is easier to play against because hands are played based on logic and for logical reasons, which helps you read them in the game.

Unpredictability is the thing to be feared—raging tilt, angry, random, out-of-harmony play—situations in which you can never be sure why a player is doing a certain thing and whether his actions are based on logic, illogic, emotions, or something else. Harmony helps everyone.

If one of your goals is to be in harmony with yourself, then it is to your logical advantage to have the whole table also in harmony.

In the martial art of aikido there is a requirement to protect one's adversary or opponent and to help him regain his balance. Terry Dobson and Victor Miller in their book *Aikido in Everyday Life* speak of it as "an insistence on responsibility for the protection of one's adversary."

This will strike some poker players as odd. How can you try to protect the very people you are trying to annihilate?

But an opponent will be less likely to try to destroy you and be more predictable if he gets the feeling you're trying to protect him in some way.

What this really means is simple garden-variety consideration and courtesy.

Protecting your adversary may be as simple as commiserating with him later when you run into him on a stairwell or in the bathroom, or just nodding in sympathy at the time, forgoing the temptation to lord it over him or rub it in in any way, or any of the usual variations of arrogance or one-upmanship. Simply put, it is politeness and respect.

Arrogance displayed in the hour of triumph will never be forgotten or forgiven.

—David Lloyd George

POKER RULE #76: Join the flow.

A person who is outside the game—a newcomer, let's say— once he has played a few times is welcomed inside, and joins the rhythm and the flow. As an outsider he may certainly win, but he is a more cumbersome presence, bulling his way through to various victories under the disapproving eye of the group. A player who has numerous enemies makes it more difficult on himself. Once this player is welcomed into the interconnectedness of the flow, a more Zen-like rhythm is reached for all players.

Good warriors lessen opponents, bad warriors increase opponents. Those who decrease opponents flourish; thereby, those who increase opponents perish.

—Sun Tzu

The relationship between you and your opponents is not a frivolous or inconsequential one. At the most basic level, without them there can be no game.

You and your opponent are one. There is a coexisting relationship between you. You coexist with your opponent and become his complement, absorbing his attack and using his force to overcome him.

—Bruce Lee, quoted in *Zen in the Martial Arts*

23

On Overconfidence, Pride, and Arrogance

When will you ever stop competing? Before you real-ize, the scenery of spring has turned to autumn. The leaves fall, the geese migrate, the frost gradually grows colder. Clothed and shod, what more do you seek?
—Zen master Fenyang

The way of the wise man is to act and not compete.
—Zen proverb

We put too much emphasis on winning, Buddhism would say, too much earnest emotion and solemn effort. How much is enough? How many victories are enough? Other worlds exist, other levels of existence and enjoyment. Buddhism views competing as the kind of straining and striving that produces self-frustrating activ-ity of the "wheel spinning" variety. It sees it as dividing up the al-ready integrated whole into parts and pitting them against one another. While competing in poker is part of the game, of course, it can be seen in a different way. It can be seen as acting—that is, simply taking *actions*. This removes the ego from the equation.

Where there is the egoity which says "I," the Buddha action does not appear.
—Trevor Leggett, *A First Zen Reader*

POKER RULE #77: Don't brag.

We commonly see the appearance of the ego in such things as arrogance or bragging. These things are usually an exercise in self-expansion that have the result, on a later occasion, of self-deflation.

POKER RULE #78: Don't rest on your laurels.

We have no laurels. The war starts over each time. Don't be overconfident of your poker skills and expertise at any time. The manner of humility is always to simply start over again, neutrally—whether it is your three hundredth poker session or your three thousandth. When you take a seat at the poker table, it should be neutrally—without ego, attitude, emotional agendas, thoughts of past successes, or other preconceptions.

If you have the idea of superiority and are proud of your ability, this is a disaster.

—Zen master Yuanwu

POWER RULE #79: Don't refer to your past as somehow giving you an edge.

"I just came from playing Hold'em for two years in Las Vegas" is typical of the kind of self-referenced edge you sometimes hear. It is generally an inner projection of oneself *to* oneself (as well as to the table), and it usually backfires. The main reason it backfires is that it doesn't really show up in the game. If anything, it may lead to a growing irritation on the part of the player that it *doesn't* seem to be showing up in the game in any way and giving him an edge. With most players, an inner belief in one's superiority is usually sufficient to cancel out any benefits of this superiority.

I once raised a player in a game of Seven-Card Stud, and he

turned to me and looked at me like I was crazy. Demented. Out of my mind. He said: "Don't you realize that I've just come from playing Stud in Reno for the last six months? You give me no respect at all with that raise."

The correct answer to this is, "No, I don't."

The lesson for this player (the one with all the Reno experience) is this: *The war starts over every time.* Every day is a new day. Skip this deep inner view of yourself, your litany of past experiences, your inner feelings of superiority, and all the rest. Because even the bad players in the game will tell you: "Hey, that's behind you—we're interested in the game taking place in front of us right now, and if you don't play well in this game, you're going to lose your money, Reno."

This "my reputation precedes me" stuff is the sports equivalent of a team suiting up and running out onto the field with the belief that just by showing up the other team will quake in its boots and concede the game. It is not a good idea to rely too heavily on this strategy. Most forms of self-pride come to grief in the game of poker.

Pride flees from the man who penetrates into the self as the light of a campfire before the rays of the sun.

—Zen proverb

POKER RULE #80: Don't become overconfident.

By overconfident I don't mean cocky, superior, pompous, self-important. I simply mean a quiet inner conviction that "probability can't get me anymore, I'm just too good."

Dismiss pride.

POKER RULE #81: Your edge is small.

Remember always that any edge you have is a small edge. It is always very subtle. Your edge is not a hammer. It is never a "hit you over the head" advantage. It is quite a small percentage. (While on the other hand, on any given day luck *can* be a big percentage in the game.) Your edge is a very subtle shading or gradation. Treat it humbly. The rule always: Humility!

When you defeat enemies in battle, it will not do to become haughty and rest on your laurels; you should be strictly prepared for adversaries at all times.

—Liu Ji

The rule is "Once you have prevailed, be as if you had not."

—*Sima's Art of War*

There is (though it is sometimes well hidden) a deep humility about great poker players. While it is true that they may often be colorful—loud, flashy, flamboyant, and so on—that is on the surface. It is a kind of "act" that takes place above the framework that they play inside of. But the humility is there, underneath the surface. (A humility that usually stems from the fact that they've seen all the worst things that can happen in a poker game.)

A casual observer may note an aura of bluster at the highest levels of poker play, but he must remember that this is tacked on to the top of the framework that contains their real play.

Success in poker, like success in any field, is based on a well-defined framework that the player operates inside of. Ultimate knowledge becomes a turning inward, to the skills inside this framework. While it is true that the individual may develop a second persona about how colorful he is (if he is a good self-promoter)—something to dazzle the boys with—the practice and experience and sweat came first and the inner discipline and humility is there.

Whenever good fortune visits a house, it is accompanied to the door by devils.

—Japanese proverb

POKER RULE #82: Be very careful when you are flush with money from a big win.

After a good-sized win or series of wins, you may get a feeling of invincibility with regard to your poker prowess. This will likely last for a period of time, an invincibility that quickly dismisses from mind the long cold spells suffered through prior to it, what a struggle it was at the time, how much toil, trouble, and, yes, even luck that it took.

A state of great ease and relaxedness generally envelops us. If you won $1,000, for instance, you might feel like, "Heck, now I can lose $200 or $300 and still be up $700." This feeling of fatness can be self-fulfilling.

Of course you are too smart to fall into this trap; you would see it coming.

Now I'm going to tell you a secret: You *will* lose that money back. I don't mean gradually, bit by bit, over time (though it could happen that way)—I mean a large, serious chunk of it, all at once. And there won't be much you can do to stop it. Bad luck will play a major part in this episode, of course. But also, maybe you are feeling just loose enough to try a few things you ordinarily wouldn't—a higher-limit game perhaps? Maybe even another game. Craps? Roulette? Whatever it is, you're not too worried because you've got this thick bankroll stuffed in your pocket—you can feel the weight of it there, like a hand grenade. But as a direct result of this attitude, your bankroll goes down, down . . . almost seemingly in answer to this carefree approach.

How am I able to say with such certainty that you will lose a significant chunk of this money back? Because things have gotten too easy—they are proceeding along quite smoothly indeed. And it's never that easy. If it is, something is wrong. Something is out of whack. And this will readjust itself in the near future.

One thing is true in poker for sure—when things are going so well that it is hard to believe what is happening, something is going to even the score around the corner.

—Roy Cooke, *Cardplayer* magazine

Smiles form the channels of a future tear.

—Lord Byron

Ten Feet Tall and Bulletproof (otherwise known as Flush with Money), is one of the most dangerous conditions in gambling—the state of being ripe for a fall is *so* ripe that it's almost off the chart.

If you are currently on this sort of winning streak, mere words cannot express what grave danger your bankroll is in. Your money is in exactly the same danger as a $5 bill in the hands of a kid in a candy store.

You must stay hungry when this point is reached—play as well and as correctly as ever. Do not relax your guard.

The problem with being up, moneywise, in poker, is no different than being flush with money in any other area of life: the temptation is to use it, to *do* something with it. It's the familiar "burning a hole in one's pocket" syndrome.

There may even be a minor pang of guilt about it—a feeling that you should give some back—which you then proceed to do, in various subtle ways. (Looser, more flamboyant play? Bigger tips? A round of drinks? Dinner's on you?)

So how do you know when to stop, when you're ahead? It's not really a question of knowing when to stop—it's more a question of buckling down and continuing to play well, not getting sloppy just because you have a lot of money, and in this sloppiness, giving it all back.

Once you come off a significant win be very wary, and *very* suspicious, from that moment on. You cannot look out too closely for what is about to happen next.

24

Steaming . . . and Other Emotions

When wrath speaks, wisdom veils her face.
—Chinese proverb

Fighting through your emotions so that you can play with a cool head may be the single most difficult thing you'll ever have to do to become a winning poker player.
—Professional poker player Lou Krieger

POKER RULE #83: Don't steam.

Steaming, in poker parlance, is what happens when your queen's-up full house loses to a king's-up full house, or when your four kings lose to four aces. The term undoubtedly comes from the fact that steam begins to come out of your ears as you watch a pile of chips and money slide across the table to another player.

If possible, don't steam. (This is easier said than done, of course.) But while the pain may be real, steaming is counterproductive.

Anyone who has played a lot of poker recognizes that these hands (*bad beats,* as they are called) are going to occur. Become annoyed. Become angry. Then forget about them. Wipe the slate clean. Resist the urge to give these occurrences a lot of emotional weight. Develop the ability to quickly reset yourself back to your normal game, and reset your passions back to zero. (The ability to go from anger and outrage to completely neutral in about ten seconds is a valuable skill in poker.)

Use the time usually devoted to steaming to go back over the hand in your mind to see if you missed anything. Did your opponent bet with a certain smoothness and authority that you missed? Could you have played your hand any other way? Could *your* hand have been read by him and nevertheless he was still betting? Did you put in an extra bet or two that you might have saved? There is always something to be analyzed. Do it neutrally. Turn steam into analysis. Recognize that these things happen.

All have the Buddha nature, but it cannot be seen when covered by the passions.

—Trevor Leggett, *A First Zen Reader*

POKER RULE #84: Don't complain when you lose.

Not complaining when you lose is not only good sportsmanship, it also has an important practical value. When you fold your cards quietly, to others around the table it becomes less memorable when you lose. And since nobody can remember you losing, you develop a silent, unspoken reputation as "the guy who never loses." This raises your stature in your opponents' eyes and makes you a more formidable player. Who wants to call a bet against a guy no one can remember losing? If they search back in their minds and can't remember the times you lost, they will be more intimidated by you. I have seen players at the table bitterly accused of never losing whom I have personally seen lose half their hands, but because they never made a big deal out of it the other players didn't remember it.

On the other hand, the player who rants and raves, who makes a big production out of losing, people file that away in the back of their minds and they stay in longer against this guy. He may encourage bets later that he doesn't want because people remember him, vividly, losing on other occasions. (Or he may encourage further bets in an attempt to get him to "go off" again.)

Finally, by not reacting to a money loss you signal something else to your opponents: your coolness as a player. (If this is how you react to losing *money,* you certainly aren't going to react to a mere change in your cards during the hand.)

POKER RULE #85: Don't be mean-spirited.

Playing poker brings out the worst in certain people—they take losses personally, act rude, get nasty, launch vendettas, and so on. They may try to rub it in when they win, insult other players and tell them in a condescending way how they should have played their hand, and so on. This sort of mean-spirited approach to the game is not particularly helpful for the player or anyone else.

The main reason for not being mean-spirited is not that it doesn't work, or because it's annoying, or that it makes poker less fun for everyone (yourself included), or that it makes you a poorer player. The real reason is this: It can get reinforced, by success. Meanness in any facet of life, if it appears to work, always runs the danger of being reached for again on subsequent occasions. It becomes a working tool. All you need to remember is that it is possible to win at poker without having a chip on one's shoulder. Many well-known pros do it all the time.

When you unleash your aggression or hostility on another person, it inspires aggression and hostility in return. The result then is conflict, which all true martial artists try to avoid. Anger doesn't demand action. When you act in anger, you lose self-control.
—Joe Hyams, *Zen in the Martial Arts*

The more he progresses the more indifferent he becomes to baseness and meanness . . . He takes it all in stride, like the weather.
—Eugen Herrigel, *The Method of Zen*

POKER RULE #86: Eliminate macho.

It is also a good rule to try to eliminate macho from your game. Few things can get you in trouble faster than this mano-to-mano stuff.

There has always been, of course, a certain gunslinger mentality to the game of poker, and like the old West, there will always be newcomers coming up in the ranks who are wilder, brasher, and more unpredictable, who will make everyone else sit back on their heels for a time. (That is, until everyone adjusts.) If possible, try to avoid getting involved in this one-on-one macho sort of thing.

Dismiss the idea that poker is a case of two gunslingers going at it head to head, one of whom is about to lose his manhood. It is more accurately seen as an exercise in long-term mathematical probability. Approach things neutrally and objectively. Doing this eliminates distorting emotions, which impede clear analysis.

If people find fault with you and try to put you in a bad light, wrongly slandering and vilifying you, just step back and observe yourself. Don't harbor any dislike, don't enter into any contests, and don't get upset, angry, or resentful. Just cut right through it and be as if you never heard or saw it. Eventually malevolent pests will disappear of themselves.
                                        —Zen master Yuanwu

POKER RULE #87: Don't develop a personal vendetta against a certain player.

Similar to the macho problem above, this is another dead end. True, there are some people who play in such a deliberately obnoxious way—players so abrasive, rude, annoying (as well as totally convinced that their ability is far superior to yours and everyone else's)—that eventually you just can't wait to stick it to them by beating them. Tempting as this is, dismiss it from mind. Continue to play *your* game, coldly, neutrally. Play against them as you would anybody else. (This *is* the best way to beat them.) Don't let them draw you off your game. Remain neutral and unemotional. Nurse the hope that at some time in the game you will get a monster hand at the same time that Mr. Mouthy across the table gets a good hand and falls into your trap. At that time set the hook and reel him in. But don't stay on bad hands trying to catch him or chase him.

Remember that certain players make a living by doing this. They use this strategy to induce other players to stay longer in a hand than they ordinarily might. You win by tuning it all out.

Don't be baited off your game.

The would-be intimidator thrives on evoking a response from his intended victim. When there is none, he quickly wears out.
—Joe Hyams, *Zen in the Martial Arts*

Learn how to be unreceptive to external forms.
—Zen proverb

POKER RULE #88: Show your opponents that you can't be baited.

If a player says: "I'm going to raise and get rid of all the bad players—all the cheapskates, the pigeons, and the shoe clerks," say: "Yeah, that's me, I'm a shoe clerk," and drop out. Show that verbally this kind of chatter has no effect on you. This removes all the power from it, and he will eventually give up on you and turn his attention to someone else.

There are blatant challenges like this that sometimes occur, but there are also challenges that operate on a more subliminal level, below your usual radar. Phrases such as "I'm going to raise them right out of their seats" may induce you to stay in when you know you should fold. Just enough of a challenge is being set so it doesn't really register. No names are being called, no big dares or challenges set down. It is all quite subtle. So you reach for your chips.

You are knowledgeable, of course, about all the obvious-type challenges, the blatant ones, but keep in mind that it's good to watch for these subtle kind, too.

———————

Just still the thoughts in your mind. It is good to do this right in the midst of disturbance.

—Zen master Yuanwu

———————

Finally, in the category of Steaming, a couple of closing remarks need to be made on the subject of whining and complaining, which seems to be a major (and growing) problem in cardrooms everywhere:

POKER RULE #89: Resist the temptation to develop a theme to the game.

A poker game is not a novel, it is not a play, it is not a movie. It is not necessary to establish a plotline or a unifying theme. ("I get low cards, then I get high cards and my hand gets wrecked, see? This happens over and over." Or: "I get second-place hands, again and again See?" Or: "Lookit—I keep getting beat on the river!" Or: "See—I start out well every hand, but then my cards go bad and I can't finish the hand.")

There are some players who seem to be under the impression that the game is a novel and it is their job to establish the plotline. They often end up developing it in such detail, in such a full-blown way, that it turns into a complete MGM production (making it ever larger and more elaborate in response to the fact that no one else cares). They flesh it out, add details, cut corners, overstate things, *bend* the truth to make the facts fit, simply in order to keep their theme consistent.

The problem with this: it is very close to whining.

(Not content with establishing a plotline some players also have to create "characters." So-and-so *always* makes flushes. So-and-so *always* hits his full houses. So-and-so always makes his low, or always wins on the last card. This is evidently an extension of coming up with a plot. These would be the characters to the story apparently.)

Just play the game. Don't dream up a lot of dark plot scenarios and accompanying characters. (Some players put so much energy and emotion into this sort of thing that they eventually talk themselves into losing. The final step often is that they put the voodoo hex on *themselves*.)

Forget all this. *Just play the game.*

A player who plays like this can be manipulated—simply by playing into his darkest fears and superstitions.* If you simply play calmly and neutrally, you will be insulated from the effects of all this type of stuff.

The game is fine. It doesn't need a plotline. It doesn't need characters.

Eight Final Reasons Not to Whine or Complain in Poker

REASON #1: You Look Kind of Silly When You Win.

You've seen him, the player who sits at the table and the whole time his mouth never stops moving:

"I never get a break . . . I always lose . . . I haven't had a hand in months . . . I never have any luck . . . I never win a hand . . ." And so on, and so on. The problem with this sort of talk is that it looks kind of silly when it is followed by a big win (say, with four aces). When a monster hand is preceded by forty-five minutes of whining, a rather sheepish look is then required.

REASON #2: Not Whining Adds to Your Personal Invincibility Quotient.

By not whining it's like the regular problems that everyone else faces in the game—not hitting the flop, having to endure cold streaks, second-best hands, and so on—don't apply to you. As a

---

*By all means encourage this in an opponent, if he shows an inclination to do it.

player, you're somehow immune to all this and don't have to suffer through it. Your invincibility quotient rises.

REASON #3: Complaining Implies That You Have Problems in the Game but Other Players Don't.

Your opponents have never lost on the river—they've never suffered a bad beat, a losing streak, or a run of bad cards. They've never had to suffer through the kinds of things you do in the game. And it is for this reason, of course, that they should listen to you. "Listen to my story, it's sadder than yours"—that's the real message here. This can be a little grating, especially to the player who is down several hundred dollars himself.

REASON #4: What Is the Whine-ee Supposed to Do? How Is He Supposed to Act?

The guy the whiner is whining *to* may find himself going up against him on the very next hand. What is he supposed to do then—drop out? Take it easy on him? Bet less? Nod in tender sympathy at the same time that he is trying to beat the guy's brains out? The whole concept goes against the very notion of correct play in the game of poker.

The bottom line: It doesn't make logical sense to seek sympathy from the very group that is trying to beat your brains out (and vice versa).

REASON #5: Whining Practically Shouts "Lack of Experience."

Long experience at the poker table and extensive amounts of playing time soon show a player that annoying losses occur all the time and are simply part of the game. It is proclaiming one's amateur status to be outraged by them.

REASON #6: Your Opponents Don't Care.

Sometime when you are in a poker game and one of the players is whining away, vociferously and endlessly, take a look at the players who are sitting on either side of him. Note the way they are staring off into space in opposite directions, like they are a million miles away. These are the players the whiner often thinks are listening to him. They aren't.

The problem here is that the players who are currently winning aren't interested, and the ones who are losing have their own problems. Certainly one of the saddest sights in poker is a player who is trying desperately to communicate his sad plight, turning first to one player, then to another (some of whom may pretend to listen, simply out of politeness, but none of whom really care), turning this way and that, trying to get someone to listen (as people on each side of him shift slightly and turn away).

The sad truth of the matter is, when we are complaining we are basically talking to ourselves—because no one else is listening.

REASON #7: It Can Set Off a Chain Reaction.

This may be the best reason of all not to complain in a poker game. It can start a chain reaction. How often have you "mentioned" something about your hand—quite innocently—only to have the guy next to you unleash an onslaught, a torrent, a verbal gusher of missed opportunities, failed outcomes, past disappointments? The fact is, if you complain, it paves the way for *other* players to start up. It opens the door. Simply mention that you "missed your draw" and watch the door fly open. The player on your left seizes the chance to describe his cards in numbing detail; the player on your right uses it as his own launching pad to recount the "worst beats he's ever had," a player at the far end tries to top them both . . . and so on. In light of this, the rule is: Don't open the door. Fold your cards without making a *single* comment. Some players are just waiting for this door to open, even a crack.

Buddhism is extremely easy and saves the most energy. It's just that you yourself waste energy and cause yourself trouble.
—Zen master Foyan

REASON #8: It's a Waste of Energy.

Ranting and raving and carrying on takes energy and doesn't change the cards or the outcome. The true champion in almost any field of endeavor is the one who conserves his energy, who paces himself, and applies it at the right time. He does not use up great raw amounts of energy at random times. He is usually seen conserving, instead, in a Zen sense.

———————

Zen practice requires detachment from thought, this is the best way to save energy.

—Zen master Foyan

———————

POKER RULE #90: If you lose the Zen, at least continue to play your cards right.

If you're going to get angry, fall into a bad mood, get outraged, lose your cool, and fall off the Zen, at least still try to play your cards right. While a Zen calmness helps you play the right cards, remember that you can also play the right cards in *un*-calmness. There is no reason a player can't be raging and fuming and at the same time still play his cards right.

25

Bad Luck and Losing

No sooner do you escape a deer than you come across a tiger.

—Korean proverb

POKER RULE #91: While being in a good mood doesn't guarantee success at poker, being in a bad mood almost always guarantees that something is going to go wrong.

It won't necessarily make you a winner if you are in a good mood, but it will almost assuredly make you a loser if you are not. The number of people who have gambled while feeling depressed, irritable, or angry, who then went on to win large sums of money could probably be counted on the fingers of one hand since time began on earth.

In short, try to play poker when you are in a good mood. Restrict yourself to times when you feel confident, alert, comfortable, and positive.

Also, if there's something you don't feel quite right about—you didn't sleep well the night before, or you were reluctant to make the long drive to the game, or you can't get in the game you wanted to play, or you're a little out of sorts, or exhausted, or whatever it is—don't play. These things have a way of coming back to haunt you in gambling situations.

Fight when full of energy, flee when drained of energy.
                    —Wei Liaozi, *Rigor of War*

POKER RULE #92: Skip the last two hours of the game.

Any experienced, longtime player can keep his game pretty well pulled together for ten hours or so. After that, a kind of general punchiness sets in. The mind begins to wander. Apathy and inattentiveness appear. Mistakes are made. (Some marathon players play for thirty or forty hours or longer.) At that point, more often than not it becomes just a bunch of players passing money back and forth groggily, everyone trying to hit something big and fluke out a late-night win. During these final hours of a game nothing is really being achieved. Drop out. Go home. Or simply cash out and sit there and listen to the chatter (which often gets more interesting at this time of night).

Disaster sometimes rolls over and becomes blessing.
                    —Chinese proverb

POKER RULE #93: Don't Panic.

"It's not over until it's over" is a well-worn cliché but it's true. As bad as things might seem, they can suddenly turn around 180 degrees. Every poker player has a story about how he was getting annihilated all night long with terrible cards, then caught good cards right at the end of the game and went home a winner. Just as dawn is peeking over the horizon you can sometimes win several big hands in a row. Don't jump to conclusions. It really *isn't* over until it's over. Don't make some sort of grand mental summation about the way things are going that precludes the good things from still happening. Stay focused, quiet, and alert. The good things can occur suddenly, and they can occur in bunches. (They can also occur right at the end of the night.)

This is part of the Zen.

POKER RULE #94: The cards will tell you how much money you are going to win.

The cards will tell you on any given night how much money you are going to win (or lose or break even). They will tell you this quite simply, by how well they are running or not running. If you think, contrary to this, that you are going to (or worse, *deserve* to) win a lot, you will probably overreach yourself. You will start pressing or overplaying. The cards will let you know the range you are going to be in; your job is to maximize it.

This maximizing of your cards may mean winning $250 on cards another player might have only won $200 on, or it might mean losing $200 instead of $300.

Don't overplay your cards. Success in poker is a rhythm; don't try to go outside the rhythm.

Your cards, and luck, good or bad, will tell you the baseline *range* you are going to be in. Your job is to get to the top of that range.

———

The world is ruled by letting things take their course. It cannot be ruled by interfering.

—Lao-tzu

———

The Personality of the Poker Player

It sometimes seems to be the case that people who are attracted to poker have *lives* that resemble (or parallel), a poker game. A list of these parallels might read like this: The suffering of some kind of slings and arrows, some brand of persecution; being ground down by events, yet having an occasional big triumph and rising above them; not terribly fond of physical work; a belief in the power of the rational mind to succeed, or make money (as opposed to back-breaking physical labor); believers in the analytical, problem-solving approach, but one also that contains a certain dash of flair; a person who likes to reduce the whole complex world to "the felt" (a small area taking place in front of them); a "simplifier," a reducer of life's complexities; an escapist; a person with a thick skin; yet a believer in hopefulness, possibilities, and good fortune, even last-second miracles; but a dark side, too—an occasional desire to "punish" (or to be punished); a belief in camaraderie; membership in cultural subgroups of one kind or other; societal mavericks or outcasts.

In short, their lives have actually been a poker game, and when they came across the game of poker itself, well . . . Eureka! They found a home . . . it was something that exactly mirrored their life.

All of the above is certainly a pop-psychology possibility, but here we would like to take up one aspect of this—the Victim.

A defective attitude can get to be your friend if you don't look out.

—Richard Ford, *Independence Day*

POKER RULE #95: Don't get in touch with your victim side.

Within every gambler is undoubtedly some buried memory of loss: the little kid whose ball was taken away; the kid who was picked last on the softball team; the kid who had his bike or his marbles or lunch money stolen by a bigger kid; the kid who the other kids didn't want around. Maybe even one motive for gambling is to replay some of these long-lost situations and relive them and have them come out a different way—to triumph, to *overcome* this inner kid. But always remember that kid is there, plus his emotions—and don't link up with him. Repudiate these rich, indulgent emotions—sad, dejected, feeling-sorry-for-yourself emotions—all still there, buried. They *do* offer a certain psychic payoff when we wallow in them. Don't be tempted. Don't tap into them.

Victimhood [is] seductive, a release from responsibility and caring . . . a weary resignation . . . a comforting self-pity.

—Dean Koontz, *Intensity*

POKER RULE #96: Don't succumb to victim thinking.

I have stated several times in this book that poker is nothing more than a long, random, statistical game. The game itself is not out to prove that you are inherently unlucky, that nothing ever goes right in your life, or that you are a perpetual victim. It is simply a mechanical, neutral, random game—nothing more. It is no more out to get you than the Spin the Wheel at a county fair is out to get you. Treat the game neutrally; try not to get emotionally involved.

POKER RULE #97: Resist the allure of failure.

Winning is a thrill, but it is actually rather one-dimensional, if we think about it. Failure, and losing, if the truth be known, are much more multidimensional. They have many more facets and dimensions to them.

If winning is Sergeant Preston of the Yukon (straight as a ramrod), and Dudley Do-Right and Billy Graham, then losing is (by contrast) Muddy Waters and Raymond Chandler and Rick from *Casablanca*. Which of these has the richer texture to it? The reason for much failure, perhaps (in all areas of life), is because this dimension of failure is more attractive in certain ways, more multifaceted than that of success. There are more emotional textures and shadings. Now, I didn't say it was more fun—just more complex and darkly multifaceted. It's more romantic, in a certain dark, fatalistic way. And if this is true, it may be an explanation for why we are sometimes attracted to it. As regards poker, you have to avoid entering this territory. One way to do this is with Zen detachment. You must resist this strange magnetic pull, the pull of "The Gambler's Blues" and "Paul Butterfield's Blues" and all the other blues when you're at the table. You must resist *enjoying* the dark side—the dark bluesy realm where you are losing money and wallowing in the wonderful comfort of self-pity. It may seem odd that we could be attracted by losing, but it does have this quality, and all poker players will know what I mean. It becomes quite easy to resign yourself and wallow in it. You must keep the focus on winning, no matter how seductive some of these darker states of mind may be.

A gem is not polished without rubbing, nor a man perfected without trials.

—Chinese proverb

POKER RULE #98: Don't give in to the death wish.

The death wish is resignation, fatalism, dejection, despair—in the face of luck repeatedly turning against us. The death wish is admitting defeat and shrugging your shoulders and throwing up your hands (generally after a string of losses) and not caring from then on whether you win or lose. The death wish is throwing money into the pot fatalistically, to punish yourself. It is saying, "I might as well keep throwing my money away at this point, because it doesn't matter anymore." It is holding your wallet up in the air and saying to the other players, "Here, you might as well take this too." It is the poker equivalent of self-pity.

The problem with the death wish is that it removes the brain's analytical, decision-making function from the equation. It also tends to magnify disasters. It takes a bad situation and kicks it up to the next level. It also misses opportunities, because its attention is so focused on the great sadness of its plight, instead. It may even miss the turn-around point—when things start changing and going the other way and getting better—so intent is it on making an airtight case concerning the sadness of its plight.

Try not to give in to the death wish. True, it can be difficult and we've all failed at times. We've all found ourselves in the midst of a cold spell so stunning, so breathtaking, so seemingly endless, a veritable Chernobyl of poker disaster, that we begin to doubt whether we are ever going to win again. We've all seen its effects on other players, too: the player who is in white-knuckle panic; the player who is silent, brooding, and sullen; the player who repeatedly leaves the table to make the melancholy trek to the ATM machine ("The Walk of Shame," as my friend Dave Joranson has labeled this). Still, even here, in the depths, we must try not to give in to it. If a disaster starts to unfold, try as much as possible to keep it under control, not exaggerate it further. Try to salvage something from the night. Play fewer hands. Scale back your involvement. Order a drink. Look around. Go for a walk. Go watch something on TV. Eat something. Go do *anything*.

POKER RULE #99: After a major poker failure occurs, resist the temptation to do something big, dramatic, and fatalistic.

Sometimes near the end of a losing session a grand dramatic gesture—a final big roll of the dice in which you risk all—can be appealing. (Anyone who has gambled for any length of time has heard someone say the following words: "Well, I might as well bet it all now and go home broke.") This is not a good attitude. A better idea is to pull back and reset. Play tight again. Return to your best game; return to the Zen. Possessing some degree of Zen-like detachment from the game is a form of protection against this type of attitude.

POKER RULE #100: Make sure you know when you're on a cold streak.

A player is angry, his face is red, his teeth are clenched, steam is emitting from his ears. He is sitting with his arms crossed, sullen, pouting. But a strange thing is happening: He is not aware of his condition. He is not stepping back from it and seeing it—and, more important, not *acting* on this information. As a result, as cold as he is, you often see him right back in there on the next hand, fighting, struggling, betting. When a player is this cold, and getting hammered this bad, he should be playing fewer hands, *not* more.

Good players can almost feel the cards changing. They know in a couple instances that they are coming up against a wall and that the next two hours may be like this. And they play accordingly. If you are on a cold streak, *notice* it. Realize that you are cold and stop fighting it. Do *not* challenge it and continue betting right into the teeth of it—daring it to get you—it will.

———————————

When the reality of power has been surrendered, it's playing a dangerous game to seek to retain the appearance of it.
—Alexis de Tocqueville

26

Examine Your Motives

Search back into your own vision—think back to the mind that thinks. Who is it?

—Zen master Foyan

Why Are You Playing Poker?

The answer appears to be obvious. To play the game, to win money. What other reason is there? But is that the real, deep-down truth? Every player should question himself about his true, underlying motives. Is he really here to play poker? Or is he here for some other hidden reason?

What, you may ask, other motives are there?

You lose sight of the original mind, and seeing the thinking, discriminating mind, take that as your own. But that is not your real mind.

—Trevor Leggett, *A First Zen Reader*

There are, in fact, numerous other motives.

- There are people who are in dire need of friends; people in search of acceptance by a group—any group.
- There are those with a deep-rooted belief that things always go wrong for them, that nothing good ever happens, who have a wish to confirm this fact to themselves (gambling works wonderfully for this).

- There is the individual who may have an inner vision of him-self as a wild, dashing riverboat gambler—role-playing—and yet another player who feels deeply insecure and is look-ing for something to raise his low self-esteem and self-worth; an occasional big pot and congratulations all around serves the purpose here.
- There is the player who believes in creating memorable, flourishing triumphs—the kind of lone-eagle, spectacular triumphs to be remembered by everyone.
- There is the person who uses poker the way people use punching bags—to get rid of the day's frustrations—and there is the person who uses *himself* as a punching bag, and employs poker to do the damage.
- There are those who are simply hooked on the adrenaline of the action, and those who are using poker as a drug to blot out thoughts and pressures—as a form of escape, from work, business, or a spouse.
- There is the retired person who is just passing the time, lis-tening to the latest jokes and gossip, enjoying the cama-raderie and the table talk.

I tell people to get to know themselves. Some people think this means what beginners observe and consider it easy to understand. Reflect more carefully, in a more leisurely man-ner—what do you call your self?

—Zen master Foyan

It ought to be stressed that none of these hidden motives are illegal or evil or bad—they may be exactly what you want out of a poker game. But the problem is, not very many of them have any relation to the task at hand: playing the game with the disci-pline necessary to win consistently.

The Temporary Motive

As if all of the above weren't enough, there is another category of motive, a subcategory we might call the temporary motive. For on a surface level, too, poker offers a myriad of opportunities to convert feelings into direct action.

For instance, feeling lackadaisical? Carefree? Generous? Irritable, impatient? Angry, tired, discouraged? Poker offers a chance to convert all these feelings into actions as well, and often, into losses. (Other temporary motives may also occur: a fight with a spouse; the rent money coming due; being angry at another player, a boss, a parking lot attendant; lack of sleep; and so on.)

Whatever *temporary* motives or emotions you possess, these, too, can (and will) be converted into direct poker outcomes at the table and will pile on top of the other more permanent ones.

In summation, there are many motives, both deep-seated and temporary. These motives can be as numerous as there are people. Some can be deeply hidden. Some can be surface and quite temporary.

Poker is a kind of Rorschach test, mirroring the personality of the player, his needs and desires. Because of this, you need to ask yourself: Why am I really at the table? Because whatever your underlying motives are, they *will* show up in the game. Your actions will filter out like little tributaries from these main premises you hold. It also distorts your game to pursue and act out these hidden goals. (To not know they exist may cause you to wonder why certain things keep happening over and over: "Why I am always ahead in chips at the beginning of the game but seem to lose them all back at the end?" for example.)

In the root and stem of your own psyche there is an accumulation of bad habits. If you cannot see through them and act independently of them, you will unavoidably get bogged down along the way.

—Zen master Yuansou

Man's character is the product of his premises.

—Ayn Rand, *The Fountainhead*

The practice of Zen stresses direct seeing into one's true nature.

Perhaps the practice of poker ought to stress a similar goal—direct seeing into one's true nature.

The question to ask is this: Are you playing poker for some reason other than to play poker?

♥　♣　♦　♠

Karma

A somewhat similar concept in Buddhism is karma. The concept of karma refers to the consequences of good actions and bad actions as they develop over time (or in reincarnation over various lifetimes, according to some Buddhist traditions). In the West, bad karma has come to mean that somebody is going to come to a bad end. But it is actually, in a narrower sense, a kind of overreaching that takes us outside the flow of normal behavior. Bad actions are ones that are in some way more artificial and inauthentic; they try too hard and by their nature "go outside the lines" of accepted behavior in an attempt to reach their goals. (It is often said of someone in poker when he is playing too loose that he is "out of line.") As a result, failure begins to occur and come back on them. There is a linking of cause and effect that occurs, between the actions we take and their inevitable outcomes.

Indeed there is nothing in the world so rigid as the law of cause and effect, or karma.

—Trevor Leggett, *A First Zen Reader*

We don't know what to call it . . . [so] we say coincidence. It goes deeper . . . You're a gambler. You get a feeling about a horse, a poker hand. There's a hidden principle. *Every process contains its own outcome.*

—Don DeLillo, *Libra*

How is your process? How solid is it? Remember, your *outcome* is contained inside it.

A bad player sits down to play. The other players all exchange a glance, knowing this player's outcome before it even occurs, before a single card has been played.

His outcome has already been decided. It is contained within his process, his game. The end and the beginning are not separate. Cause and effect are one.

The oneness of cause and effect is not a mere theory, but something actually experienced. Cause is effect: effect is cause; they are not two!

—Trevor Leggett, *A First Zen Reader*

This is similar to the effect that hidden motives have on our play.

What we sow is what we reap.

27

Mastery: Expertise in Sight

We have seen the need for Zen calm and detachment in poker; the need for practice, rhythm, discipline, and humility. The starting point, as always, is knowing the game well, perfecting the process—and only then adding psychology, self-control, game selection and other skills. Expertise will then be in sight. In Zen terms, we will have entered the *flow*.

When Zen practice is completely developed, there is no center, no extremes; there are no edges or corners. It is perfectly round and frictionless.

—Zen master Hongzhi

Humility and self-effacement occur. In our quietness we may even cease to be a perceived threat. Modesty and humility will be in evidence. It might seem that such a person would be conspicuous and stand out in a crowd, but in fact the opposite is true. We become more invisible in the landscape. Those looking at us would probably not notice us.

In those who attain Zen, mental machinations disappear, vision and action are forgotten, and there are no subjective views. Zen adepts just remain free, and are imperceptible to anyone, either would-be supporters or would-be antagonists.
—Zen master Yuanwu

The player, in a sense, has become a different person. This may not be outwardly apparent to an onlooker. His movements may indicate something about him—both at the poker table and away from it. The manner in which he does everything indicates something.

A man who has attained mastery of an art reveals it in his every action.
—Samurai maxim, in *Zen in the Martial Arts,*
by Joe Hyams

No matter how much calm or detachment, how much Zen we possess, however, we will still falter at times because we are human. In our humanness we may emerge from a poker game perfectly at peace, but then wish to do grave bodily harm to another driver on the freeway on the way home. We are never quite fully and completely there—at the end of the process. It is ongoing, difficult to master completely. It is nothing that ever finishes. We are always on the journey.

You begin to understand that warriorship is a path or a thread that runs through your entire life. It is not just a technique that you apply when an obstacle arises or when you are unhappy or depressed. Warriorship is a continual journey.
—Chogyam Trungpa, *Shambhala:*
The Sacred Path of the Warrior

If we persist, however, we eventually enter through the door of a realm where greatness of many different kinds resides, where the truth of many different games, sports, and disciplines overlap. We will join and become an accepted member of a long-standing fraternity.

We may have risen higher than we would have imagined when we started the journey. Progress took place silently. We discover that the secret was not far away after all; it was actually close at hand the whole time.

The sixth ancestor of Zen said to someone who had just been awakened, "What I tell you is not a secret. The secret is in you."

—Zen master Fayan

Final Comment

A critic of the worlds of both poker and Zen might say that both of them share an "insulating oneself from life" factor (you might almost say a "running away from life" factor). A mental realm is taken up in both cases that can be used for escapism.

And there is little doubt that either one, in the wrong hands, can be used as an escape from real life, its tribulations and vicissitudes. Both share a kind of self-absorption—one trained inward, one trained outward (table-ward?).

Both could also be accused of keeping regular emotions at arm's length by seeking another level of psychic rewards—poker externally, Zen internally (by retreating inward). Such a critic might say poker can no longer see the moonlight; Zen sees only the moonlight.

Gambling itself, as an activity, can be a thrill—often a deeper thrill than many nongamblers ever experience. Thrilling as it may be, however, in many ways it is still quite one-dimensional as an activity. Across the board, it does not have the richness and nuance of larger life (that is, life beyond gambling).

In this regard, in order to achieve the true Zen of poker, it is probably necessary to achieve some sort of overall balance in our larger life. Little is gained if we arrive at the true Zen of poker, while the rest of our life is a shambles. (And there are players like this.) Eventually, something will begin to disintegrate in our poker game as well.

Another danger of poker is a kind of one-dimensionality. Such a tunnel of focus is required to maintain one's edge that this tunnel can begin keeping other things out (or *everything* out). Being "in action" becomes paramount. Play enough poker and it becomes possible to walk through a sunny day completely blind, without even seeing it. Our eyes look—but no longer see—a sunset. A spring day. An autumn day. A winter scene. These are things you pass *through* on your way to the poker room—things merely "off to the side," no more real than as if they were projected on a movie screen. (Two signs of this condition: time going by—often in large amounts—poker is very time-intensive; and a growing inability to cope with real or everyday life—a feeling of being left out of the usual things everyone else is involved in.)

The best poker players—the very best, world-class players when they are in action—are machines. They are cool-headed, intuitive, impassive, imperturbable, and relentless. While having attained this apex of a high art, there is a danger of other things being left out. Clearly, such a state of affairs contains the risk of running counter, at some point, to life itself. If we are playing continuously, day and night, and as a result have finally arrived at this fine point in poker, the possibility exists that our larger life may be out of whack. And at some point this will catch up to us—*and* to our game. A more advisable path is probably to work on having one's whole life in balance. For this reason, in certain situations, the meaning of Zen in the larger sense may override Zen in the narrower sense.

In any case, it is always good to remember that there is another world out there beyond the poker-room windows—of nature and love and art and music and people, a world of pheasants in fields on autumn days and daughters graduating from college and bright faces on children in playgrounds, a wider world, one more well rounded and multidimensional than that of gambling. The best poker players, in their wisdom, know this truth, too.

Appendix 1

Zen and Tournament Play

Poker tournaments are held throughout the United States every year, and in recent years the number has grown at a phenomenal pace. In a poker tournament, there is usually a *buy-in*—whether $30, $50, or $100—and the player is given *tournament chips* to play with, for instance, $2,000. The tournament then proceeds until each player loses his chips, or wins. (If it is a rebuy tournament, he can rebuy more within a designated time period.) Money, trophies, and other prizes are handed out to the top finishers. (In the 1999 Tournament of Champions, for example, each player reaching the Final Table of the tournament received a new car. And each year at the World Series of Poker—where the buy-in for the tournament is $10,000—the winner receives $1 million in cash.)

Tournament play may be said to produce both more and less stress than regular play; more because of the one-time-only, winner-take-all, big-event nature of a tournament, and less because we are playing with tournament chips and can freely take some chances we wouldn't if it were "real money." (We are protected on the downside: the worst that can happen is we lose our buy-in.) The stress of tournament play is therefore of a slightly different nature.

A good portion of achieving a Zen-like state of composure in a poker tournament is simply a matter of having a realistic view of one's chances.

In a tournament with 200 other players, for instance, one's long-shot possibilities of winning are just that, a long shot. (Picture cutting cards with 200 people.) Even if you managed to survive until you were among the last 40 finalists, and 160 other players had busted out, you would still be a 40:1 underdog to win the tournament!

It's also entirely possible to play in a tournament and win only a hand or two—or none at all—if your cards are bad enough. Or it's possible to be the chip leader one minute and be out of the tournament shortly thereafter. Or to be sailing along in fine shape and hit several excellent hands, all of which lose—and then have to watch the rest of the tournament from the sidelines.

In the light of these possibilities, the Zen suggestion on tournament poker is this: Do not become too heavily invested emotionally in the outcome. Luck is a big factor in these events. (Or, as Amarillo Slim once put it: "There's an awful lot of tall timber you have to get through to win one of these things.") Play your best, accept what happens, enjoy yourself, take the outcome that occurs.

The player can use this awareness of the long-shot aspect to attain stillness and composure, and to focus on the task at hand. (Which is where his focus should be, anyway.) He should play aggressively and confidently, certainly come with the attitude that he is there to win, but keep in mind his realistic chances.

Other Tournament Comments

1. Survival is a top priority. "Don't be stubborn" is a good rule of tournament play. It is more important to gracefully withdraw from a hand and live to fight another day than it is to try to show opponents you can't be pushed around. If the signals start to make it clear that you are beat, you *must* get out. Unlike in a regular game, the chips are irreplaceable (in a regular game you can simply go into your pocket and buy more with your own money). Another way of saying this is: Don't get married to the hand. Don't hang on to a sinking boat, even if it was a wonderful boat to begin with. If you encounter what seems like real resistance, take it seriously—fold. You can't win a tournament if you are no longer in it. Pride and obstinacy can be fatal in tournament play.

2. The more frequently you push your whole stack in, the more likely it is that one of those times you will lose it and be eliminated. Try to restrict such situations to as few as possible.

3. Try to keep your confrontations, whenever possible, to opponents who have the small stacks (for the simple reason that these players will be more reluctant to call your bets, as well as limited in raising you back). This becomes even more important near the end of the tournament.

4. If it is a rebuy tournament, play looser and more adventurously during the rebuy period; tighten up when the rebuys end.

5. Try to observe, and get a line on, your opponents. Who are the worst players at your table? Who are the best? Who plays in a predictable manner? Who is staying too long on marginal hands? What kind of cards are the players turning over? How tight, timid, or aggressive are the players on your immediate left? Will they defend their *blinds* (antes), or can you steal the blinds on them?

6. Don't forget to factor in position to your play. Always make a note of where the dealer button is.

7. Make a decision before the tournament starts to play only certain (good) hands. Make other strategy decisions beforehand, too: "I won't be blinded out; I'll take a stand and go all in on a good hand first, before that happens," for example. Such premade decisions save regrets, and second-guessing, later on the drive home if you bust out.

8. Don't give up. Don't resign yourself to losing at any point and throw in the towel (or your few remaining chips). As hopeless as it may seem, numerous stories abound about players who were down to their last chip and came back to win a tournament.

9. A final comment: Many players don't play tournaments; they restrict their play to live action only. By doing so they're really missing an opportunity to get a different take on the game, to see it from a different angle. It's a good way to use a different part of one's brain, applied toward the same game. It is also a way of taking a brief mental vacation from the mental rut of playing in continual side action.

Appendix 2

Notes on Zen and Poker Computer Software

Recent years have seen the introduction of poker computer software as a learning aid, to practice and perfect one's game. The appearance of this software has radically changed the face of the game. While possessing many advantages, however, the software is not perfect, and there have been some criticisms. In general, these criticisms fall into three categories:

1. One-dimensionality
2. The human factor
3. The differences between the computer game and a live game in a real cardroom

1. One-Dimensionality

The criticism here is that poker computer software cannot imitate all the many complex factors occurring in a game. The computer opponents, in particular, tend to play in a one-dimensional way; they have no flexibility of response against you as an opponent. In addition, they can't learn from past hands, and unlike real players, don't adjust their strategy.*

---

*For an excellent discussion of this subject, the reader is directed to *The Poker Player's Software Guide,* by Shay Addams.

2. Human Factor Criticisms

This criticism usually includes the adage, "poker is a people game, not just a card game." In other words, computer software might be good for learning to play the cards in poker, but it can't tell you how to play the people. An example would be human opponents who change their game deliberately from time to time, or those who go on tilt; the use of *table image*; the absence of common elements of basic psychology (no smiles, stares, grimaces, head shakes, looks of disgust, fakes, feints, and so on). In short, the reading of tells—an important poker tool—cannot be practiced with software.

3. Computer Versus Live Game Criticisms

The quiet home atmosphere—where poker software is usually practiced—is much more conducive to optimum play than the noise, stress, and commotion of a real cardroom. In the comfort of one's home there are no misdeals, angry outbursts, card-throwing tantrums, spilled drinks, muttered accusations, veiled threats, and so on.

Other Criticisms

It's difficult to remember exact computer point values in the heat of a hectic poker room. It's also easier to bet fictional money on a computer screen. In addition, there is also a tendency to play much quicker on a computer, the hands zipping by at a high rate of speed, a much different pace than in live-game play.

These are a few of the disadvantages. There are some advantages, however.

Some of these are:

Software Advantage #1: Software helps in what is known as game theory.

Game theory is the analysis of situations where information is incomplete. Playing thousands of hands on computer software helps the player intuitively fill in the missing information with a pretty accurate sense, thus allowing a good educated guess at the correct odds in various situations.

Software use can also help the player determine what "average luck" is (and "average" cards)—a very valuable thing to know—and where he stands in relation to this.

Software Advantage #2: Software practice raises your certainty level.

Software practice has a way of giving assurance and conviction to your betting—a self-confidence that is transmitted to the other players. This can often be intimidating, and is a self-assurance not only missing from other players (who are often more hesitant) but puts them on the defensive.

Software Advantage #3: It keeps you humble.

Software practice keeps the player humble, keeps him from getting an exaggerated idea of himself as a player, because it is rooted in impersonal play. It brings us right back down to earth if we don't stay focused and alert. The software doesn't care about a player's ego, his past record, how well known he is, how many tournaments he's won, his personal feelings regarding his own great prowess, or anything else. It can throw a series of bad hands at you that will have you sweating, muttering, and cursing. Software thus deflates the "big head" syndrome and forces us to keep our game on track.

Software Advantage #4: Software practice helps achieve detachment and indifference.

This may be one of its primary uses. Through the playing of thousands of hands, it demonstrates clearly that outcomes come and go, that they matter only in the long run, and that it is not productive to become emotionally involved in individual hands. This is a valuable lesson and helps the player proceed with a certain measure of indifference in the live game—a viewpoint that keeps him detached as well as making him harder to read.

Software Advantage #5: The player is taken through the same range of emotions as a live game.

Critics of poker software often overlook the fact that most of the same *emotions* occur in software play as in a live game. Thus, it can be used to master oneself—a benefit whose value cannot be overstated. By responding to various obstacles that appear, the player *moves in and out of emotional states.* This is extremely good and valuable practice.

Software Advantage #6: Software can be used to work on yourself, as well as the game.

The fact is, after a certain point, the player already knows the game. It is often more helpful, therefore, at this point, to use software to work on yourself—self-control, calm, composure, concentration, and so on.

We cannot put ourselves in too many situations, too often, where our moods are called forth and challenged (frustration, anger, annoyance, disbelief). Using software to get into these situations (and out of them) again and again allows us to develop emotional resources for live-game play.

Software Advantage #7: Software can be used to bring poker knowledge to the forefront of consciousness again.

We often hear the phrase, with regard to computers: "I'll bring it up on the screen." Well, this is a primary use of poker software too—to "bring it up" on *our* screen—to put it in the forefront of our consciousness and get ourselves back into the groove. The player can use the software to "recall" the game, to front-load it into his immediate thoughts and bring himself up to speed for a live game to come. This brief trial run provides an opportunity to make mistakes ahead of time and to stave off dangerous tendencies in our play—playing too loose or staying too long in a hand, for instance—thus correcting them before the live game starts.

Two Cautionary Notes Involving Poker Software

1. Don't practice when you're tired.

Occasionally, deliberate practice on poker software when you're tired can be helpful (to see if you can maintain the Zen). Such times occur in live games, too—usually late at night. However, don't practice *too* much when you're tired, because wrong lessons can be learned and strengthened, bad habits reinforced. No real learning is taking place when you're tired. (In fact, *unlearning* may very well be taking place.)

2. The computer game takes place at high speed.

This is another trap of computer software—the ability to play at lightning speed. Then the player gets in a live game and becomes impatient because the game seems to unfold in slow motion (complete with long dealer-shuffling gaps in between) in comparison to the game he's become accustomed to on the computer screen.

A second problem is that the software gets you through cold spells quicker. You can fold hundreds of terrible hands in a short time—the equivalent of untold countless hours of play in a live game. Thus, our *emotions* need to downshift in order to compensate for the difference in tempo of play. Software's ease of folding bad cards can be a dangerous model for the way a cold spell is going to feel in a real game. It's much longer, slower, more painful, and the suffering is more drawn out.

Final Note

Very important, with regard to poker software, is the amount of time we practice. If we overplay, the game starts to become lifeless, boring, and flat; we lose interest and begin to play mechanically, not really paying attention. Eyes glaze over and a kind of burnout occurs. Lackluster, halfhearted play takes place.* (While this may seem harmless, in actuality it is not much different than playing when tired or when drinking—the end effect is the same. A lack of interest occurs that catapults us quickly back into the amateur ranks.)

How much practice is too much? Or not enough?

This is an objective decision, but it is also a *subjective* one; it goes by how you feel. The player must develop a sensitive personal "antennae" for when he is right on that edge. If you feel you are playing too much (on the software), then you probably are. It has primarily to do with your interest in the game.

There is almost nothing more important than this "interest" in the game—an eagerness, a sharpness, even excitement of it. It keeps an edge to the player's game, keeps him learning, noticing, and, above all, *caring*. Whenever this caring stops, indifferent play begins.

Proponents

Proponents of poker software sometimes make the mistake of forgetting that the human brain is a computer, too—able to assimilate facts and information at lightning speeds unrivaled by anything at Microsoft or IBM. Rest assured, each player at the table has his own computer with him—and as long as it is assimilating and weighing facts correctly, learning the right lessons and constantly adjusting, it will be an opponent for you not to underestimate.

Critics

To critics of poker software, we might say this: While software does have its disadvantages, it is good not to judge too harshly, because of its relative newness on the scene. It is well to remember that nothing involving computers ever gets worse as time goes on—it always gets better.

---

*Any player who doubts this can prove it to himself quite easily—simply by overdoing it. Practice poker software for several hours beyond what feels right. You will soon see how impatience and irritability set in, followed quickly by boredom, indifference, and poor play.

Bibliography

Addams, Shay. *The Poker Player's Software Guide.* Tucson, AZ: Pocket Rockets Press, 1996.

Berger, K.T. *Zen Driving.* New York: Ballantine, 1988.

Boldt, Laurence G. *Zen Soup.* New York: Viking, 1997.

Braverman, Arthur, tr. *Warrior of Zen—The Diamond-Hard Wisdom Mind of Suzuki Shosan.* New York: Kodansha America, 1994.

Cleary, Thomas, tr. *Sun Tzu—The Art of War.* Boston: Shambhala, 1988.

Cleary, Thomas, tr. *Mastering the Art of War—Commentaries on Sun Tzu's Classic.* Boston: Shambhala, 1989.

Cleary, Thomas, tr. *Zen Essence—The Science of Freedom.* Boston: Shambhala, 1989.

Connolly, Cyril. *The Unquiet Grave.* New York: Harper and Brothers, 1945.

Cooke, Roy. "Real Poker: The Cooke Collection." Las Vegas: Mike Caro University of Poker, Gaming and Life Strategy, 1999.

Dobson, Terry, and Miller, Victor. *Aikido in Everyday Life—Giving in to Get Your Way.* Berkeley, CA: North Atlantic Books, 1978.

Canty, Kevin. *Rounders.* New York: Hyperion, 1998.

Csikszentmihalyi, Mihaly. *Finding Flow.* New York: Basic Books, 1997.

Dostoyevsky, Fyodor. *The Gambler.* Boston: Charles E. Tuttle, 1994.

Ekman, Paul. *Telling Lies—Clues to Deceit in the Marketplace, Politics, and Marriage.* New York: W.W. Norton, 1985.

Ford, Richard. *Independence Day.* New York: Alfred A. Knopf, 1995.

Froug, William. *Zen and the Art of Screenwriting.* Beverly Hills, CA: Silman-James Press, 1996.

Griffith, Samuel, tr. *Sun Tzu—The Art of War.* New York: Oxford Univ. Press, 1963.

Hagen, Steve. *Buddhism, Plain and Simple.* Boston: Charles E. Tuttle, 1997.

Herrigel, Eugen. *The Method of Zen.* New York: Pantheon, 1960.

———. *Zen in the Art of Archery.* New York: Random House, 1981.

Høeg, Peter. *Smilla's Sense of Snow.* New York: Dell, 1995.

Hyams, Joe. *Zen in the Martial Arts.* New York: Bantam, 1979.

Jackson, Phil. *Sacred Hoops.* New York: Hyperion, 1995.

Jones, Rex. *The Railbird.* Hollywood, CA: Gambling Times, 1984.

Kabat-Zinn, Jon. *Wherever You Go There You Are.* New York: Hyperion, 1994.

King, Winston. *Zen and the Way of the Sword.* New York: Oxford Univ. Press, 1993.

Koontz, Dean. *Intensity.* New York: Random House, 1995.

Leggett, Trevor, tr. *A First Zen Reader.* Rutledge, VT: Charles E. Tuttle, 1960.

Leonard, George. *Mastery.* New York: Dutton, 1991.

Mackay, Harvey. *Dig Your Well Before You Get Thirsty.* New York: Bantam, 1997.

———. *Swim With the Sharks Without Being Eaten Alive.* New York: William Morrow, 1988.

May, Jesse. *Shut Up and Deal.* New York: Doubleday, 1998.

McMullan, Jim and Levin, Michael. *Instant Zen.* Boston: Charles E. Tuttle, 1994.

Norretranders, Tor. *The User Illusion.* New York: Viking, 1998.

Norris, Chuck. *The Secret Power Within—Zen Solutions to Real Problems.* Boston: Little, Brown, 1996.

Pirsig, Robert M. *Zen and the Art of Motorcycle Maintenance.* New York: William Morrow, 1974.

Ratti, Oscar, and Westbrook, Adele. *The Secrets of the Samurai: A Survey of the Martial Arts of Japan.*

Roberts, Wess. *Leadership Secrets of Attila the Hun.* New York: Warner, 1985.

Schiller, David. *The Little Zen Companion.* New York: Workman, 1994.

Shoemaker, Fred. *Extraordinary Golf—The Art of the Impossible.* New York: Putnam, 1996.

Shulman, Neville. *Zen in the Art of Climbing Mountains.* Boston: Charles E. Tuttle, 1992.

Sokoloff, Arthur. *Life Without Stress—The Far Eastern Antidote to Tension and Anxiety.* New York: Broadway Books, 1997.

Stabinsky, Miron, with Jeremy Silman. *Zen and the Art of Casino Gaming.* New York: Summit, 1995.

St. Ruth, Diana and Richard. *The Simple Guide to Zen Buddhism.* Folkestone, England: Global Books, 1998.

Suzuki, D.T. *Zen and Japanese Culture.* Princeton, NJ: Princeton Univ. Press, 1959.

Trungpa, Chogyam. *Shambhala—The Sacred Path of the Warrior.* Boston: Shambhala, 1984.

Watts, Alan. *The Way of Zen.* New York: Random House, 1957.

Yong-chol, Kim. *Proverbs, East And West.* Elizabeth, NJ: Hollym International, 1991.

Acknowledgments

Every student has many teachers, and I am indebted to those who taught me, for the lessons in this book. These include:

The gang in Blanchardville, for whom poker is an endless game; the Monroe game: Ross Lancaster and John Gobeli, Roger Seffrood, Greg "Duck" Wuetrich, Max Wyssbrod, Angelo Andrias and Ken Rufer; Gary Stamm, Justin Stamm and Fritz Amacher, Markus Meier, Greg Syse and Bob Golackson; Todd and Fred Wirtz, Max Voelkli, Duane Hanson, Mary Ryan, Richard Kundert, Buffy, Cutty and Buck; John Huber and John Wagner; Buck and Richard Tschanz; Bill Buehler, Bob Flanagan, Clark K. and Werner Z . . . Tom Bacon and Ginger R.

The LaCrosse players: Fred, Tom, Gilby, Oz, Kaz, Squirt, Ken Peterson, and Charlie Kline.

Joe Willi and Kenny King and the cast and crew of Diamond Jo's riverboat: Kurt, Kevin, Jimmy, Leon and the dealers and personnel on the Miss Marquette Mississippi riverboat.

Special thanks to: Schmitty and Launa; Jeff Conway of Old Smokey; Carl Wenger, Hugh Richardson, Clint Bellmeyer, Wayne Tyler, Dean Jackson, Don Roberts, Ray Babb, Bob McGranahan, Mike Palm and Bill Schultz.

Also, players and friends: Bob Wittman, Dave Juergens, Craig Stamm, Ken Kruser, Mary and Pete Massey, Rick Reinke, J.P., Dan Waisman, Bill Dearth, Dewey Weum, Robin S., Dennis R., Jeff, Louis, Mike, Rich, Audrey, Duane and Dan, Gloria T., Greg J., Jimmy N., Sony, Frank F., Portage Dave Bailey, Dave Stoltz, Tom H., Big Al, Jimmy Ryan, Lyle, Don, Steve, Dennis, and others too numerous to mention. They know who they are.

In the poker industry: June Fields, Linda Johnson, Michael Konik, and Peter Ruchman of the Gambler's Book Shop in Las Vegas; in the publishing industry, Joel Fishman and Kevin Lang of the Bedford Book Works, world's greatest agents, and Deborah Brody of Dutton for effort above and beyond the call.